Answers in a Time of Miscarriage

Bethany Kerr

ANSWERS IN A TIME OF MISCARRIAGE

Copyright © 2011 by Bethany Kerr

All rights reserved. No part of this book may be reproduced or transmitted in any form or by any means without written permission from the author.

Scripture quotations are from The Holy Bible, English Standard Version® (ESV®), copyright © 2001 by Crossway, a publishing ministry of Good News Publishers.

Used by permission. All rights reserved.

ISBN 978-0-615-43853-5

Printed in USA by **Silver Trumpet Publishing**

Table of Contents

Introduction..7

Acknowledgements...10

Questions and Answers about Miscarriage..........12

- ♥ I feel like the pain will never end..12
- ♥ I don't feel supported by my husband..................................12
- ♥ I feel guilty because I was not able to find my baby............14
- ♥ In what ways can I memorialize my baby?.........................15
- ♥ Am I crazy for feeling so bad about my miscarriage?..........15
- ♥ What does the Bible say about unborn children?................16
- ♥ Do babies who die go to Heaven?..17
- ♥ How can I help others who are going through this pain?....18
- ♥ How will I be able to tell people?..21
- ♥ Can I have a memorial service?...22
- ♥ Did I lose the baby because I didn't have enough faith?.....22
- ♥ Some people I know have said some very hurtful things....23
- ♥ Why would God allow me to suffer like this?......................23
- ♥ I don't think that I am feeling enough emotion..................24
- ♥ I have been so snappy and angry lately..............................25
- ♥ Why doesn't anyone seem to understand?.........................26
- ♥ How long should I wait to try again?..................................26
- ♥ Was this miscarriage my fault?...27
- ♥ How do I tell the children?..27
- ♥ I had an ectopic pregnancy...29

Physical Questions..30

- ♥ My HCG levels are rising, but only slightly.........................31

- ♥ *The doctors told me I have a blighted ovum*..........................31
- ♥ *What generally causes a miscarriage?*...............................31
- ♥ *Does spotting always mean miscarriage?*............................35
- ♥ *Will I be given my baby's remains after having a D & C?*.....35
- ♥ *What should I expect if I choose to miscarry at home?*.......36
- ♥ *Is it safe for me to have a natural miscarriage at home?*....39
- ♥ *How can I physically heal after a miscarriage?*...... 39
- ♥ *How long do you bleed after a miscarriage?*........................40
- ♥ *What do I do with my baby's remains?* 40
- ♥ *Do you know anyone who has ever had a public funeral*... .41
- ♥ *I want to have a natural miscarriage*....................... 43
- ♥ *What is a D & C and what are the risks?*.............................43
- ♥ *Are D & C's necessary?*...44
- ♥ *I have a "missed miscarriage" and need a D & C*................45
- ♥ *If I am bleeding a lot, could my baby still be okay?*............46
- ♥ *How can I find a pro-life physician in my area?*..................47
- ♥ *If I think I am miscarrying, when should I call my doctor?*...47
- ♥ *How does my doctor know that I have miscarried?*............47
- ♥ *Can the birth control pill cause a miscarriage?*...................47
- ♥ *Will it be painful (natural miscarriage)?*................. 49
- ♥ *Will it be painful (D & C)?*...49
- ♥ *How long will the bleeding last (natural miscarriage)?*.......50
- ♥ *How long will the bleeding last (D & C)?*..............................50
- ♥ *When can we start trying again?*............................. 51
- ♥ *What is a Chemical Pregnancy?*..51
- ♥ *How can you know you have had a Chemical Pregnancy?*..51

♥ *What is a "Missed Miscarriage"?*..........52
♥ *If I am having a missed miscarriage, how long*..........52

STORIES ABOUT MISCARRIAGE..........54
   Sara's Story..........55
   Penny's Story..........58
   Amanda's Story..........60
   Rebecca's Story..........62

ECTOPIC LOSS STORIES..........70
   Rheanon's Story..........71
   Heather's Story..........78
   Jan's Story..........86

MEN'S STORIES..........91
   Jason's Story..........92
   Ken's Story..........95
   Steve's Story..........97

MY MISCARRIAGE STORY..........101
HOW TO COMFORT MOTHERS..........158
WHAT NOT TO SAY..........159
   In Their Own Words (what didn't help)..........164

WHAT TO SAY..........169
   In their own words (what helped)..........170

ENCOURAGEMENT..........177
   Poems..........178
   Articles..........185
   Quotes..........190

RESOURCES...191
    Books...192
    Websites..195
    Songs...197
    Scripture...200
FETAL DEVELOPMENT...203
    Seven Weeks..204
    Eight Weeks...205
    Eleven Weeks..206
    Twenty Weeks..207
ROWAN'S FUNERAL PICTURES...208
PICTURES OF MY BABY, BLESSING KERR.......................209

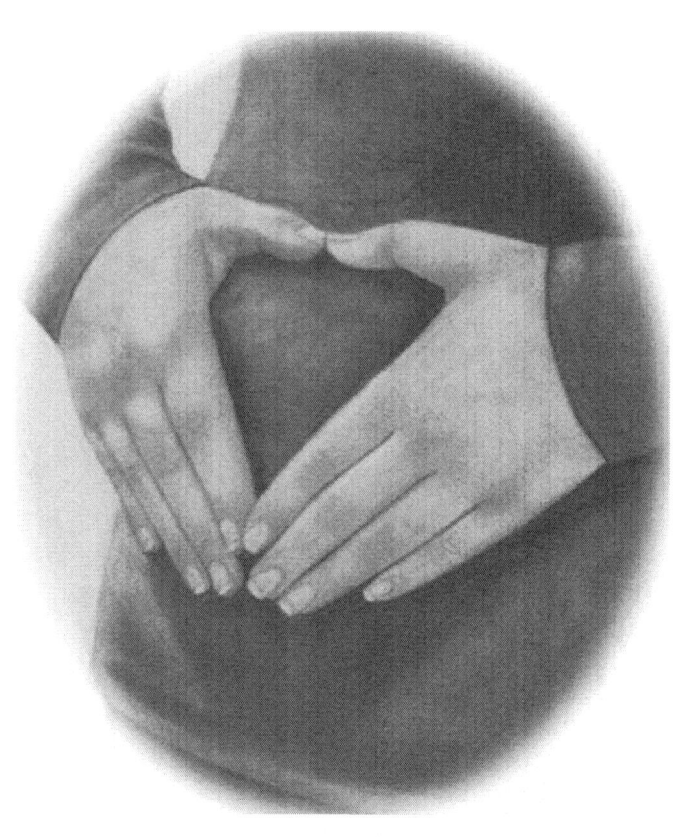

Introduction

Between the months of February and March of 2007, I suffered my first of two miscarriages. I posted about my experience on my website and shared pictures of my baby to others with the hopes that my story and these pictures would help someone else out there who might be going through the same thing.

Since that time, I have received numerous emails and phone calls from women who have been comforted by the story and the pictures of my baby. In fact, so many have contacted me that I felt I should compile a book, a resource for women out there who are suffering from the loss of a baby.

I hope that this book will help women out there who need encouragement; so that they will know and understand that it is okay for them to grieve.

If you have gone through a miscarriage recently, chances are you don't have many people to talk to about it. You may feel that you are "crazy" or "weird" for feeling so strongly about a person you have never met before, or who has only been in your womb for a short period of time, and you never have really had the chance to "meet" face to face. You may have people telling you that you're overreacting, or you may have people who expect you to "feel better" in a matter of weeks. You may have tried to share your feelings with people who want to avoid talking about it. These people might attempt to cheer you up by making light of it - unknowingly making your pain even greater.

No matter what the case, I want you to know that you are not alone.

Some people may say things that make you feel guilty or ashamed for having such strong emotions and grief. There is absolutely nothing abnormal about you or about your grieving. If you have had a miscarriage, you indeed lost a unique, special human being that was created in God's image. You have every right to grieve that loss.

A VERY SPECIAL THANKS TO...

Allison Almand	Louise Wolf	Myung Hee Guderian
Sandy Maclean	Jennie Lee	Connie Baugh
Jill Stanek	Linda Martin	Saundra Behringer
Carla Stream	Autumn Hanson	Kyra Hill
Valerie Ryan	Melanie Kendall	Jane Adkins
Sarah DeGroff	Dana Patterson	Dana Perrow
Michelle Monk	Tracy Parsons	Leigh Anne White
Penny Greene	Ken Bridges	Tera Wolf
Loretta Rizzo	Steve Schweigert	Shelly Ard
Rheanon Short	Alicia Raulerson	Lauren Pope
Sandi Bender	Sheri Maple	Bethany Powell
Jason Bender	Catherine Scott	Jessica Sundholm
Sara Newman	Jan Richardson	Kristi Bennett
Jacinda Montalto	Rebecca Hegarty	Maria Vassilieva
Julie Chatten	Heather Baker	Tiffany
Lisa Chandler	Myah Walker	Cris
Amanda McCleskey	Lindsey	Marcie
Margaret Delle	Tammy	Kay
Jennie Lee	Jane	

and countless others who helped me in so many ways. Thank you from the bottom of my heart for all of your help, prayers, and insight. I could never have created this book without you!

Most of all, thanks to my husband, James Kerr, who supported me and encouraged me to finish this book from the very beginning.
I love you.

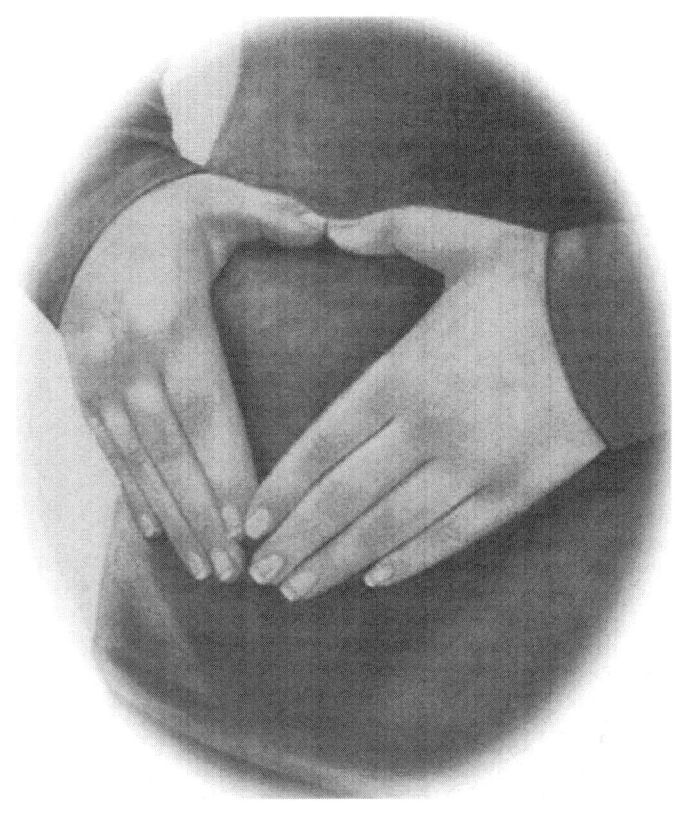

QUESTIONS AND ANSWERS ABOUT MISCARRIAGE

♥ **I feel like the pain will never end. How long can I expect to feel this way?**

The pain after a loss does become easier to bear over time, but sometimes it feels like it will never end. Some studies have shown that about a third of women can still have depression up to six months after their loss.[1]

The "expected" time for a woman to grieve really hard is 3 months, and after this, the feelings typically become less severe. However, everyone is different. Some women will continue to feel pain, even up to a year later. Some will feel "better" within just a couple of months. Some women will be fine one day, and burst into tears the next, or think they are "over it" after a few months, then when the due date of their child comes, they sink back into a depressed state.

Regardless of how early along you were in pregnancy, please know that your feelings are valid and there is nothing wrong with the feeling of a deep sadness over your loss. Please do not let anyone pressure you into "getting over it" sooner.

Ecclesiastes 3:1-4

To everything there is a season and a time to every purpose under the heaven: A time to weep, and a time to laugh; a time to mourn, and a time to dance.

♥ **I don't feel supported by my husband.**

It may make you feel somewhat better to know you are not

---
[1] *(American Journal Of Psychiatry February 1996; 153:226-230)*

alone in this. As sad as it is to say this, it is actually very rare for a woman to actually feel supported by her husband during this time.

However, this does not always mean that your husband does not care about the miscarriage, or feel the pain or grief that you feel as well. A man who sees his wife in pain will usually seek to help her feel better. He may sometimes try to say things like, "Just try not to think about it so much.", or "Just stop dwelling on it.", thinking that this is helping you (when in reality the words wound you deeply). Your husband may be completely unaware that he has even hurt you at all.

He may not be talking to you much because he does not want to "make you cry". He may feel that talking about the miscarriage or expressing his own grief about the loss may send you into a deeper depression. Nothing could be further from the truth. Talking about your feelings is very healing (most men don't understand that talking about your feelings, no matter how bad they are, is very healing).

On the contrary, not talking about them, and not feeling free to express your grief, can actually deepen your depression and/or make it last longer.

Be sure to communicate to your husband that while you appreciate everything he's trying to do for you, what you really need is someone to talk to. You need someone to lend a listening ear, someone to just be there to say; "It's going to be okay." Express to him that he doesn't even necessarily need to say anything… that just taking the time to sit and listen to your feelings would help you very much.

You may even be able to get him to talk about his own feelings. If not, please be willing to give him time. He may be holding in his grief in order to be strong for you.

If you feel that your husband truly doesn't care at all, please take the time to pray for him, and as difficult as it may be to do, forgive him. Holding in anger and resentment for him will only worsen your grief and may hurt your marriage. God can change his heart. Give him time and try to forgive him. If he is unsupportive, you can journal your feelings about the miscarriage, and/or express them with a friend.

Read stories of miscarriage from the father's perspective on page 91.

♥ I feel guilty because I was not able to find my baby.

I am so very sorry to hear that you had to go through this. I understand how painful it is to not be able to find your baby that you miscarried. (I was not able to find the baby from my second miscarriage, and that was very hard for me as well).

It is so difficult when you want to be able to see and hold your baby one time before letting go, but are not able to.

Sadly, finding the baby is not always a possibility. Please know that this is not your fault and please keep this thought in mind if this is the situation you are in.

I have included in this book, pictures of my little baby, Blessing, who died at nearly 7 weeks after conception. You can see them in the picture section of this book. I hope that these pictures will help to give you some of the closure that you are seeking. Perhaps they will help you to know with certainty that what you lost was a significant, tiny human being.

You can still have a memorial for your baby. See the section titled "In what ways can I memorialize my baby". This will give you ideas on how to do this.

❤ In what ways can I memorialize my baby?

You can make a box filled with any memories that you have of the baby. Examples may include:

- Your positive pregnancy test.

- A letter (or email) you receive from a friend congratulating you about your pregnancy. (Or even emails or letters that you received after your loss).

- A poem or message you wrote for your child.

- A necklace with a pendant on it, a bracelet, a pin, or something else that you can wear every day to remember your baby by.

- Reach out to others who are going through the same pain.

- A name for your child. You do not have to name your child anything that is gender specific, if you were too early to know…

❤ Am I crazy for feeling so bad about my miscarriage?

No, you are absolutely not crazy for feeling this way. You lost a unique individual; your very own little child. Your child was significant and valuable, regardless of the stage of pregnancy when you suffered your loss.

♥ What does the Bible say about unborn children?

The Bible many times speaks of the significance of life in the womb- it is consistent in affirming that there is no essential difference between born and unborn child. Each possesses a soul and is created by God for a specific purpose (even though sometimes, we may not understand what the purpose was).

Psalm 139:13-16

"For you formed my inward parts; you knitted me together in my mother's womb.

I praise you, for I am fearfully and wonderfully made. Wonderful are your works; my soul knows it very well.

My frame was not hidden from you, when I was being made in secret, intricately woven in the depths of the earth.

Your eyes saw my unformed substance; in your book were written, every one of them, the days that were formed for me, when as yet there was none of them.

Isaiah 44:2a

"Thus says the LORD who made you, who formed you from the womb..."

Jeremiah 1:5a

"Before I formed you in the womb I knew you "

Luke 1:41- 44

And when Elizabeth heard the greeting of Mary, the baby leaped in her womb. And Elizabeth was filled with the Holy Spirit, and she exclaimed with a loud cry, "Blessed are you among women, and blessed is the fruit of your womb! And why is this granted to me that the mother of my Lord should come to me?

For behold, when the sound of your greeting came to my ears, the baby in my womb leaped for joy.

Psalm 127:3

Behold, children are a heritage from the LORD, the fruit of the womb a reward.

Isaiah 44:24a

"Thus says the LORD, your Redeemer, who formed you from the womb."

Galatians 1:15

"But when he who had set me apart before I was born, and who called me by his grace."

♥ Do babies who die go to Heaven?

Based on *2 Samuel 12:22, 23*, I believe they do:

"He [David] said, "While the child was still alive, I fasted and wept, for I said, 'Who knows whether the LORD will be gracious to me, that the child may live?'

But now he is dead. Why should I fast? Can I bring him back again? I shall go to him, but he will not return to me."

David specifically said that he would one day go to meet his child (in Heaven), but that his child would not be able to return to him while he was on earth.

If you are worried that this passage does not include unborn children as well as born, please take a look at *Luke 1:39-45*.

"And when Elizabeth heard the greeting of Mary, the baby leaped in her womb. And Elizabeth was filled with the Holy Spirit" (*1:41*)

John the Baptist, who was an unborn baby at the time, recognized that his (also unborn) Savior was with him, and responded "with joy".

This clearly shows how God clearly recognizes unborn children as possessing souls.

I found these passages to be very comforting when I lost my babies to miscarriage. I know that I will meet them one day.

❤ **How can I help others who are going through this pain?**

One of the most important things you can do to help someone going through the same pain as you is to listen to him/her when they talk to you about the miscarriage. Be there for them when they need you. They need to know that someone truly cares about how they feel.

Sometimes it is difficult knowing what to say, or how to "be there" in this kind of situation. You may desire to "cheer her up", but most of the time, being "cheered up" is not what a grieving mother needs or wants. She needs to be allowed time to grieve. Be willing to listen to her as she tells you about her pain. Sometimes a simple "I'm so sorry", "I love you", and a tender hug are the best ways to respond, as she pours out her feelings to you.

Be willing to still talk about the baby; avoiding discussing the baby may hurt her more. Mentioning the baby will probably bring her to tears, but this is not a negative thing. Understand that her tears are not because of you. She is crying because it is a natural part of the grieving process; she misses her child. She will be grateful to know that someone else remembers her baby and confirms that the child is not simply a 'figment of her imagination'.

There are other ways you can help her. Try to think of things that might have helped you during your time of grief, and give her things that you wished friends had given you.

Here are some other ways to help:

- Offer to come to her house and help her organize, clean, or tidy up.

- Bring prepared food to her house.

- Offer to baby sit her other children.

- Give her and her husband a gift card for a restaurant so they can have a night out.

If you make a commitment to do something to help, be sure that you will be able to keep that commitment.

Some ideas for encouragement:

- Bring her flowers.
- Bring her a rose bush or a small tree that she can plant for the memorial of her baby.
- Bring her a pretty journal for her to write her thoughts in.
- Give her a book on healing after miscarriage. (There is a listing of books that can help on page 192).
- Make or purchase a necklace, bracelet, or other type of jewelry for her to wear as a memorial to her baby.
- Buy her something personalized, with the baby's name on it.
- Buy or make her a pretty memory box for her baby.

Rom. 12:15

"Rejoice with those who rejoice, weep with those who weep."

♥ How will I be able to tell all the people I know that I have lost the baby?

There are some ways to tell friends and family members about your loss without having to confront them face to face (if this is a fear for you).

One option would be to ask your husband, mother, etc, or a close friend to help tell others for you (my husband offered to do this for me when I miscarried the first time, and it really helped).

Another option is writing a letter, and sending it to everyone who knew you were pregnant. The letter can say anything you'd like to say, including whether you'd like to have time alone or if you could use a friend to stop by and check on you every once in a while.

Sometimes it will be inevitable that you will run into someone who doesn't know about your miscarriage, and they will ask you innocently, "How is your pregnancy going?" at the worst possible time. You may feel like you don't want to burden them with your problem. In my situation, this happened a few times, and each time, I wanted to run away and cry.

However, I found myself facing my worst fears, at least once, and I choked out the words, "I lost the baby.", but I was unable to say it without crying. I did burst into tears and tried to walk away. The person who I spoke with stopped me, and sat down with me. We talked about what happened, and she expressed her deepest sympathy. She encouraged me with kind, caring words and Godly advice.

Even though I hadn't really wanted to talk to anyone about my loss, it did make me feel much better to "get it out" and to have someone speak to me about it. I went through the rest of the day feeling as though a burden had been lifted off my shoulders.

So if someone comes to you asking you about the baby, it may just be that God is bringing that person to you, to encourage you.

♥ **Can I have a memorial service, even if I was not able to see my baby?**

A memorial service for your baby is one of the best things you can do to start the healing process. It can be very helpful in giving you the closure that you may not have had since you did not see the baby. It can help you recognize the reality of the loss of the baby you were welcoming into your life.

While a traditional memorial service is acceptable, many people actually prefer to have a private memorial service, right at home. My husband and I chose to have a memorial in our backyard. Of course, it all depends on what you feel is best for your family.

♥ **Did I lose the baby because I didn't have enough faith in God?**

No. The Bible does not reassure us that as Christians, faithful to God, that we will not experience pain, sickness, heartache, or loss in this lifetime on earth. In fact, it states quite the opposite.

The Bible says that the "rain falls on the just and on the unjust" (*Matt. 5:45*). All of us, young and old, rich and poor, good and evil, will experience suffering, pain, loss, and heartache as long as we are on earth. However, we know that as faithful Christians, all things will work together for good.

♥ **Some people I know have said some very hurtful things to me regarding my miscarriage. How should I react?**

If a person hasn't experienced a loss, they might say insensitive things without understanding the impact of their words. Most of the time, the best way to respond is to ignore these remarks. Try not to take their words to heart. I realize this is easier said than done, but there is really no way for someone to truly understand what you're going through unless they have experienced it for themselves. Dwelling on their comment is not going to help you heal. Just remind yourself that some people just won't understand, and that is okay.

If you believe their intent was to comfort you, then try to be as understanding as you can and let the comment go, or gently let them know how it made you feel. Most of the time, friends will apologize for a remark that was unintentionally hurtful.

♥ **Why would God allow me to suffer like this? I wanted this baby.**

A friend of mine sent an answer to this question that I hope you will find very encouraging:

"This was the hardest question BY FAR for my husband and me. I mean, we prayed so hard for the baby we lost in June of 2007. To be honest, we felt, a bit betrayed, because we went into God's word and reminded Him of His promises, and His answer was still "no". Ouch.

So through much prayer, I finally realized that God <u>had</u> answered our prayer for a child. Though its life on this world was very short, that child is alive for eternity.

In the expanse of eternity, 8 weeks or 80 years are inconsequential. We had also prayed (as we do for all of our children) that God would make them strong men/women in His image and that they would grow to honor Him. We believe that this prayer was answered when He took our children before birth, because they will not face the temptations and sins of this world.

It still hurts, but I believe that God had a purpose for even the shortest life here on Earth, and we are so thankful that we got to spend even a short while with our little ones in heaven."

♥ I feel guilty because I don't feel that I am feeling enough emotion - I feel numb.

You may have seen other women reacting to their miscarriages in a very emotional way, and you may have wondered, "Am I a bad mother for not feeling that way? Is there something wrong with me? Why am I not crying, too?"

Please don't feel guilty. The numb, detached feeling you describe is a normal reaction, and is nothing to be ashamed of.

Also, the very fact that you feel guilty for feeling this way suggests that you may be feeling a lot more than you realize.

♥ **I have been so snappy and angry lately…I don't know why I can't seem to stop.**

It's really difficult coping after a miscarriage. No one else seems to recognize the pain you are in. You don't want to burden anyone with your problems. Most of the time, you aren't given any answers as to "why" it happened. You don't have time to really sit and reflect on your feelings, as you still have many responsibilities. There are still dishes to do, bills that need to be paid, and children to be fed. All of these things are demanding your time and attention while you need time to heal.

Anger and irritability are obviously a normal reaction to the stress that you are dealing with.

Here are some ideas on how to cope with those feelings of anger. These can help you to feel much more positive so that you can get through each day:

1.) Write your feelings down.

2.) Find a support group for parents who are dealing with loss by miscarriage. You can find many such groups online. It is such a help to be able to share your feelings with someone who understands what you are going through.

3.) Exercise. Even just a little exercise can really help lift your spirits.

4.) Make sure that you are getting enough sleep every night. Sleep does much to help relieve the mind and body of stress.

5.) Allow yourself some time to cry...don't continually fight back tears. If you have children, see if you can find someone to watch them for a couple of hours so that you can spend a little time alone for this. Also, if it makes it any easier, listen to some soft music, or watch a sad movie and let the tears come. After a good cleansing cry, you'll feel a lot better.

♥ Why doesn't anyone seem to understand what I'm going through?

Unless someone has actually experienced a miscarriage, it's almost impossible to truly understand what it is like. It is good to surround yourself with people who understand what you have been through. Try finding a miscarriage support group in your area by calling a doctor, your OB, or your local Crisis Pregnancy Center. You can also find discussion forums online where you can find support from others who understand exactly what you are going through. (Some online discussion forums are listed on page 195)

♥ How long should I wait to try again?

When you feel physically and emotionally ready, there is no reason you should not be able to try again. Some doctors will recommend that you wait one to three cycles before trying again. One reason for this is that it is easier to calculate the conception date if you have had a menstrual cycle. It is a good idea to wait at least one cycle so that you can be sure that your miscarriage has completed and that there is no tissue remaining inside

♥ **Was this miscarriage my fault?**

No!

The majority of miscarriages happen due to a chromosomal abnormality, something that would be impossible for you to control.

It doesn't matter if you have done any or all of the things that have the potential to cause a miscarriage...that doesn't mean you caused your miscarriage. Many women make unhealthy lifestyle choices, and still manage to carry their babies to full term.

Also, many women who have taken ALL precautions and have kept themselves as healthy as possible still miscarry!

Therefore, just because you did some things that can potentially cause miscarriage, it doesn't mean that you actually caused your miscarriage to happen by doing those things.

♥ **How do I tell the children?**

If your children knew you were pregnant, I personally believe that the best thing that you can do for your children is to be straightforward and honest about what happened. Children understand much more than we many times give them credit for. If we don't tell them, they will still know something is going on.

I waited a full year to tell my children about my miscarriage. At the time, I felt that they weren't able to handle that information emotionally (I think that secretly I also felt that I wouldn't be able to tell them without bursting into tears, and I didn't want them to see that).

The more I think about it, the more I believe it would have been good for them to be involved. That way they could have known how much it grieved me to lose their baby sister or brother, and would have been a part of it at the time it happened.

After I finally decided to tell them about the miscarriage, I was surprised at how well they handled the information. They wanted to know the name of their sibling, and why she/he died. Their Questions included, what happened to the baby afterward, and many more things. I answered all questions as honestly as I could, explaining to them how much I loved baby Blessing, and wished that he/she could be here with us. I told them about how we buried our baby under the weeping cherry trees in our yard. I showed them the pictures that I had of the baby, and the ultrasound. They gave me a hug, told me that they were sorry that Blessing had to die. I told them that our baby was safe in Heaven, and that it is a beautiful place and that Blessing is very happy there. We will see Blessing again one day.

Weeks later, I assumed wrongly that they had completely forgotten about our talk.

Out of the blue one day, Bonnie (my daughter) asked me, "Mom, why did Blessing have to die?" I was caught off guard by the question but was able to answer her and tell her that I didn't know the answer to that, only God does. I explained that one-day we will know. I gave her a hug and let her know that I missed Blessing too.

And on another occasion, my son Caleb said, "I wish that Blessing could be here with us. I know he would have been so cute, just like Noah!" I agreed with him and he got a hug.

I really think that talking about it together has brought us closer together.

♥ **I had an ectopic pregnancy...I don't feel like anyone understands what I am going through- not even those who have had a normal miscarriage.**

While I have never personally had an experience with an ectopic pregnancy, I have met many ladies who have experienced loss from one.

The normal feelings that one generally feels after an ectopic are somewhat different than the feelings after a miscarriage, although the end result of each is the same- the loss of a unique individual created by God.

Please see the Ectopic Loss section of this book. In it, you will find stories from different women who have experienced an ectopic loss. It is my prayer that these stories will give encouragement, hope, and comfort to you. It will also remind you that you have nothing to feel guilty about. I hope that their words will help you to know that you are not alone, and that your feelings are completely normal.

Physical Questions

By no means is this a comprehensive list of questions and answers, but I hope that it will help to answer many of the questions that women ask after having a miscarriage, or while dealing with one.

Important note*: I am not a medical professional. The information contained in this book is from my personal research, from talking to various doctors and nurses, and from discussing this issue with my own OB. Please seek the advice of your physician or other qualified health provider for all medical problems, treatments, or with any questions you may have.*

♥ **I had a blood test done and my HCG levels are rising, but only slightly (not doubling). Am I having a miscarriage?**

It is possible to have slow rising HCG levels and carry the baby to term. Unfortunately, slow rising HCG levels can also be an indicator that you are in the process of miscarrying. The only way to know for sure is to have your doctor continue to monitor your levels and see if they continue rising or if they begin to drop.

♥ **The doctors told me I have a blighted ovum, and that this means there never was a baby. Is this true?**

No, it's not true. In the case of the blighted ovum (also called *anembryonic pregnancy*), an egg has been fertilized, just as in any other pregnancy. Once the egg is fertilized, it is no longer an egg but a complete human being. The baby simply doesn't develop past implantation.

♥ **What generally causes a miscarriage?**

The majority of first trimester miscarriages are not explained. Doctors usually assume that these losses are caused by a chromosomal abnormality. Most chromosomal problems are unlikely to recur and are not caused by anything the parents did.

There are some situations which can make your risk for miscarriage more likely, and some of those situations include:

Hormone imbalance

Progesterone is the hormone that helps prepare the uterus for implantation. When levels of the hormone progesterone are low, it can cause a miscarriage. Your doctor can prescribe progesterone for you to take early in pregnancy if they find that your progesterone levels are low. This will help reduce the chance of miscarriage.

Diabetes and other illness

If you have properly controlled diabetes, your chances of miscarrying are no higher than average. However, poorly controlled diabetes does make miscarriage much more likely. It is very important to keep your diabetes under control as well as possible while pregnant. Your doctor will want to monitor you more closely during pregnancy if you have diabetes.

Other illnesses which are linked to miscarriage include high blood pressure, rubella (German measles), lupus, and some sexually transmitted diseases, such as herpes simplex and chlamydia. Problems associated with these illnesses during pregnancy can be many times prevented with good prenatal care.

Cervix/uterus abnormalities

Physical problems with your uterus or cervix during pregnancy can increase the risk of miscarriage. Some of these abnormalities include:

Uterine fibroids – abnormal growths (non-cancerous tumors) in the uterus. A doctor can perform different tests, including an ultrasound, MRI scans, cat scans, and X-ray to detect fibroids.

Some of the treatments for uterine fibroids make it impossible to become pregnant again, so be sure to discuss the alternative options with your doctor. Some treatments include focused ultrasound (non invasive treatment which targets tumors with high-frequency sound waves), myomectomy (surgical procedure which removes tumors without damaging healthy uterine tissue), hysterectomy (removal of the uterus), and different medications.

Incompetent cervix - when the cervix is unable to remain closed during pregnancy.

An incompetent cervix can be caused by a previous D & C procedure, an abnormality in the cervix from a birth defect, or even damage from a previous difficult birth. If you have any of these risk factors for an incompetent cervix, your doctor can determine whether you have one by performing an ultrasound or a pelvic exam. Treatment for incompetent cervix is a procedure called cerclage, in which the cervix is sewn closed. The stitches are removed in the third trimester to prevent problems during labor.

Septate uterus – a uterus that is divided into two cavities.

A septate uterus can be diagnosed by ultrasound, a hysterosalpingogram/HSG (injects dye into the fallopian tubes and uterus for an x-ray to attempt to detect any abnormalities), or a hysteroscopy (inserts a tiny telescope into the cervix to see inside the uterus). Treatment is surgery which removes the septum that is dividing the uterus.

Asherman's syndrome – scar tissue formed inside of the uterus.

Asherman's syndrome can be diagnosed in the same way as a septate uterus: through an HSG or a hysteroscopy.

Treatment frequently involves breaking up the scar tissue

through an operative hysteroscopy, then inserting a balloon into the uterine cavity (this is left in for 7-10 days). This is followed by antibiotics to prevent infection.

Immune system problems

Some immune disorders which can be a risk for miscarriage include:

Antiphospholipid antibodies – These antibodies can cause blood clots in the placenta that slow down or completely block the baby's blood supply. You can have your blood tested for these antibodies, and if the levels are found to be high enough to cause harm in the pregnancy, Heparin or Aspirin (blood thinners) might be prescribed.

Natural killer cells – These are usually an important and helpful type of cell, preventing one from getting infections and cancers. Their purpose is to seek out and destroy harmful cells in the body. However, in some women, these cells get "confused" and see the embryo as an invader (like a cancerous tumor) to the body. They then multiply and attach themselves to the embryo and kill it in the same way that they would kill a cancerous tumor.

Your blood can be tested in order to determine if natural killer cells are a cause for miscarriage. A typical treatment for this is IVIg infusions (an intravenous drug that suppresses the immune system).

Antinuclear antibodies – these are cells that attack the center of other cells in your body. Sometimes they can mistake normal cells for an intruder and attack them. This can cause illness or inflammation. Antinuclear antibodies can cause the area around the unborn baby and/or around the placenta to become inflamed, which can result in miscarriage. Your blood can be tested to determine if your antinuclear antibody levels are a risk for miscarriage. A typical treatment for this problem is Prednisone, (a corticosteroid which helps to suppress the inflammatory process).

♥ **Does spotting always mean miscarriage?**

No. About 20 percent of women will experience spotting during the first trimester without any pregnancy complications. A light spotting can indicate implantation (when the embryo attaches itself to the uterine wall), or it can be the result of sensitivity in the cervix after intercourse. Sometimes, however, it can indeed be an early sign of miscarriage, so be sure to contact your doctor if you experience spotting.

It is important to note that there is a difference between light spotting and bleeding. If the color of the blood is bright red, that is bleeding. If the color of the blood is brown or light pink, that is considered spotting. Also, spotting consists of a small amount of blood, but bleeding can soak a sanitary napkin.

Bleeding at any time during pregnancy can indicate potential problems, so it is important to tell your doctor anytime you are experiencing bleeding.

♥ **Will I be given my baby's remains after having a D & C?**

This is a very difficult question to answer. The *last* thing I ever want to bring up when talking to someone about miscarriage is abortion, but unfortunately, whether you will be given your baby's remains has much to do with the abortion laws in your state. (Please skip the rest of this section if you do not want to know any more).

Though completely unfair and insensitive to those who have lost their unborn children, in places where abortion is legal, a baby is not considered legally a "person" until the "age of viability" (which could be counted anywhere from 20 to 24 weeks, depending on your state).

Because of this, if a D & C or D & E procedure is done, the fetal remains will be considered "medical waste" instead of a human being, and will be discarded. It hurts me just to type those words, but sadly, it is the law.

You will be able to keep your baby's remains if you miscarry at home.

♥ What should I expect if I choose to miscarry at home?

If you have had a "missed miscarriage", and choose to miscarry naturally, you may start miscarrying within hours of the doctor's diagnosis. On the other hand, you may have to have to wait up to a few weeks before it begins. A study from 2002 found that 70% of women who had chosen to miscarry naturally had completed their miscarriage within 14 days of the doctor's diagnosis. [2]

---

[2] Luise, Ciro, Karen Jermy, Caroline May, Gillian Costello, William P. Collins, and Thomas H. Bourne, "<u>Outcome of expectant management of spontaneous first trimester miscarriage: observational study</u>." *BMJ* 2002. Accessed 23 Apr 2008.

You might find yourself asking yourself all kinds of questions, such as "How long will this take? What if the baby is really still alive? Am I *really* going to miscarry? I still feel pregnant. Were the doctors wrong?"

Time seems to go so slowly when you are waiting, because you just don't know if it will happen the next day, or a month from now when it will happen- not to mention, you don't know what to expect when it finally *does* happen!

If you know beforehand what to expect, it makes the waiting much easier. Every woman experiences miscarriage differently, but I hope that the following will be helpful in giving you some idea of what to expect:

Typically, a natural miscarriage will begin with a light spotting which lasts a few or several days. This spotting gradually changes to a bright red bleeding. Along with the bleeding, you may begin experiencing cramps.

You might notice the cramping coming, then going- very much like labor contractions. Many women, however, miscarry without any physical pain.

Depending on how early you are in pregnancy, you may only notice bleeding with blood clots. The baby might be too small to be seen with the naked eye.

If you are further along (several weeks), you might pass some gray tissue (placental or fetal tissue), along with large and/or small blood clots.

Some women will pass the gestational sac and baby at once- some will pass the baby without the sac, and sometimes unfortunately, the baby cannot be found at all. If you are unable to find your baby, please do not feel guilty- sometimes they are just too small to see.

Many women are not informed of what they might see when they miscarry. Many women miscarry while on the toilet. When they see the baby, they are so shocked and scared that they panic and flush the toilet. If this has ever happened to you, please know that you did nothing wrong. You did the best you could with what information you had and with the circumstances you had to deal with.

I heard one wise woman say, "Before this ever happened, your baby was already in Heaven with Jesus."

When the baby has been passed, many women will feel guilty or ashamed at the thought of wanting to open the gestational sac to see their baby. This is a perfectly normal thing to desire to do, and does not make you morbid or strange. It is a natural desire for a mother to want to see her child after she has miscarried. It may even help you to find closure.

On the other hand, it is also normal to *not* want to look, and there is nothing wrong with that either.

If the miscarriage is complete, the bleeding should last anywhere from several days to a few weeks. Length of bleeding can vary from woman to woman. The bleeding should generally not be any heavier than the heaviest day of a period.

If you are concerned that you are bleeding too much, or too long, it is always a good idea to get in touch with your doctor.

♥ Is it safe for me to have a natural miscarriage at home?

According to the 'Journal of Family Practice' and other medical organizations, a woman can safely wait to miscarry naturally if she:

1) does not have a fever
2) has stable vital signs
3) has no excessive pain
4) has no excessive bleeding

If you meet these four criteria, waiting before having a D&C or to have a natural miscarriage is a reasonable option.

If you do not meet these criteria, you could be at risk for infection and should seek help immediately.[3]

♥ How can I physically heal after a miscarriage?

•Try to rest as much as possible, and avoid any strenuous physical activity.

•Eat healthy, well balanced foods to help your body recover more quickly.

•Continue taking prenatal vitamins or a regular multi-vitamin.

•Try to avoid eating refined sugars and junk foods as much as you can.

•Use pads, not tampons, for bleeding after miscarriage, and try

---

[3]This information found on
http://www.misdiagnosedmiscarriage.com

to abstain from sexual intercourse until your body has healed. (this reduces the odds of developing an infection).

♥ How long do you bleed after a miscarriage?

The duration of the bleeding will vary from woman to woman, but usually the bleeding will last about two to three weeks. Anything longer should be reported to a doctor so that they can rule out the possibility of an infection or incomplete miscarriage.

♥ What do I do with my baby's remains? Can I bury him/her?

(The information below was written by Sandy Maclean, a miscarriage law expert.)

Each state has its own laws on burial, and each city has its own ordinances on burial. The sad fact is that miscarried babies *legally* have no personhood, so therefore don't really fall under burial laws/ordinances as persons. Miscarried babies are not generally given any type of birth or death certificate.

Therefore, burying a miscarried baby in a yard technically does not break any state laws or city ordinances. Please check with your own state/city to find out what you are allowed to do (this is an unfortunate task to have to check into at the time of a loss).

Some cities have allowed land to be dedicated to burying stillborn and miscarried babies. St. Paul has a beautiful cemetery for all of the little angels to be buried together. Some churches have dedicated areas where they allow stillborn and miscarried babies to be buried.

If the remains are cremated, no casket is required (depending on the age of the baby, cremation may or may not be an option. If the baby is too small it will virtually evaporate during cremation. If the baby is large enough to cremate, some funeral homes will do it for free and provide an urn. There are many websites that sell small urns designed specifically for the remains of miscarried babies.) If the family wants the baby buried intact, the funeral home would provide a small container that meets state guidelines for a cemetery burial.

Women can get direction from the funeral home or hospital bereavement organizations on how to handle these issues. Most funeral homes will charge what is minimally acceptable to do what is right for the family.

Many large hospitals are now keeping all of the babies together for mass burial and will have dedication ceremonies once or twice per year. Families can participate in these ceremonies to honor their babies.

There is so much inconsistency regarding this issue. Women just need to be encouraged to *ask*.

♥ Do you know anyone who has ever had a public funeral for their miscarried baby?

Yes. One person in particular, Amanda McCleskey, was kind enough to share her story for this book, along with pictures of the funeral she and her husband held for their baby, Rowan, who passed after 12 and a half weeks in the womb.

I hope that these pictures and their story will help encourage others who might want to do the same but are afraid to for any reason:

> "Our pastor came to the hospital to share some hope with us, and to just grieve with our little family. He helped us map out what we wanted for the funeral, as we had never walked this path before.
>
> At the hospital a 'memory box' was given to us. It was the perfect size for Rowan, and so he was buried in that box. It was donated to the hospital by a group of women from Central Florida who prepare and donate the boxes as a ministry. I knew I wanted to bury the baby, and I knew I wanted it to be in a cemetery.
>
> We did some digging and found that Matt's great-grandmother was buried in a cemetery near our home, and once we contacted the cemetery they were more than happy to work with us. They allowed us to bury our sweet Rowan on top Matt's great-grandmother's plot. A tiny square of earth was removed for Rowan, and we buried him Friday, August 21, 2009.
>
> Our pastor gave a brief message, and we played several worship songs. There were so many people there, we were shocked. God has been so good. So many lives have been touched by our little angel.
>
> Since losing our baby we have been on the rampage for information of healing and hope. Miscarriages touch so many lives, and we are determined to bring the hope of Jesus to those who have lost and do not know Him."

You can read more about Amanda's story on page 60 or by visiting her blog at http://thisgirl-amanda.blogspot.com/.

♥ **I want to have a natural miscarriage, but I need to know how much bleeding is too much. When should I seek help?**

If you are soaking one pad in one hour, feeling light headed or weak you need to consult your doctor soon as possible. Soaking 3 or more pads in one hour is a sign that you probably need to go to the ER.

♥ **What is a D & C and what are the risks?**

D & C (dilation and curettage) is a procedure that involves expanding the passage of a woman's uterus so that a thin, sharp instrument can scrape or suction away the lining of the uterus.

A D & C will generally be planned for incomplete miscarriages, when the uterus has not pushed out all of the fetal or placental tissue inside it.

Some situations will make D & C more risky, and your doctor will likely avoid giving you a D & C if you have a pelvic infection, a blood clotting disorder, or other serious medical problems.

A risk directly after the procedure is infection. Signs of an infection include fever, heavy bleeding, severe cramps, or a foul smelling vaginal discharge. These should be immediately reported to a doctor so that they can be treated with antibiotics.

Other complications include the perforation of the uterus, puncture of the bowel or bladder, and scarring of the uterus leading to a condition called Asherman's Syndrome. The symptoms of Asherman's Syndrome are irregular, light, or absent menstrual periods, infertility, and recurrent miscarriages. (In some cases, the scar tissue can be removed, but 30 percent of women who acquire Asherman's Syndrome will remain infertile after treatment).[4]

A D & C procedure (especially two or more) may cause future pregnancy complications, such as ectopic pregnancy, placent previa[5], and cervical weakness. It may risk premature birth in future pregnancies[6].

❤ **Are D & C's necessary?**

A D & C is not always necessary after or during a miscarriage. About half of women who miscarry choose not to go through the D & C procedure. Most women who have miscarried naturally are able to do so successfully.

According to the research printed in the Journal of Family Practice:

_____

[4]*Learn more at http://www.ashermans.org*

[5]*Dilation and Sharp Curettage (D & C) for Abortion – Web MD (I apologize for the term abortion being used- the D & C is a procedure used for both miscarriage and abortion.)*

[6]***BJOG*** *2009; 116:1425–1442. DOI: 10.1111/j.1471-0528.2009.02278.x. Induced termination of pregnancy and low birthweight and preterm birth: a systematic review and meta-analyses. Shah P, Zao J on behalf of Knowledge Synthesis Group of Determinants of Preterm/LBW Births.*

"More than 80% of women with a first-trimester spontaneous abortion have complete natural passage of tissue within 2 to 6 weeks with no higher complication rate than that from surgical intervention (strength of recommendation [SOR]: A, based on multiple randomized controlled trials [RCTs] and cohort studies).

"Expectant management is successful within 2 to 6 weeks without increased complications in 80% to 90% of women with first-trimester incomplete spontaneous abortion and 65% to 75% of women with first-trimester missed abortion or anembryonic gestation (presenting with spotting or bleeding and ultrasound evidence of fetal demise) (SOR: B, based on multiple cohort studies).

"There is no difference in short-term psychological outcomes between expectant and surgical management (SOR: B, based on RCT).

However, there are indeed situations where a D & C might be necessary:

"Women experiencing spontaneous abortion with unstable vital signs, uncontrolled bleeding, or evidence of infection should be considered for surgical evacuation (SOR: C, expert opinion). [7]

♥ **I was told I have a "missed miscarriage" and need a D & C. What if the doctor is wrong and the baby is still alive?**

Usually, the doctor determines that the baby has passed away by seeing no heartbeat on the ultrasound, or by checking the HCG levels. The doctor will generally recommend D & C if you have a missed miscarriage, but will usually allow you a certain period to wait it out and see if you can miscarry

---

[7]*Unfortunately, the word "abortion" rather than "miscarriage" is used to describe pregnancy loss in many medical journals.*

naturally, if you so choose. (You can ask for pain medication to help ease any cramping during the miscarriage).

After a few weeks if your body has still not started the miscarriage process, or if you have an incomplete miscarriage, they will probably want you to do the D & C. The doctor will be able to tell whether your miscarriage has been completed on its own by checking your HCG levels.

Doctors can be wrong and there have been cases of miscarriages being misdiagnosed. You can read about hundreds of such cases at http://www.misdiagnosedmiscarriage.com. [8]

If you have been told that there is no heartbeat, it might be a good idea to wait at least one week (unless you are showing signs of infection or other complications) and then have a follow up ultrasound to verify.

If you decide to go ahead and schedule the D & C, please ask for a second ultrasound first because sometimes the baby's heartbeat will show up at the last minute.

❤ If I am bleeding a lot, could my baby still be okay?

In the first trimester, bleeding may not be a sign of a problem. Approximately 20 - 30 percent of women experience bleeding in the first trimester, and about half of those women do not miscarry. [9] In the second and third trimester, however, bleeding can possibly point to a serious complication. Please

---

[8]*Specifically http://www.misdiagnosedmiscarriage.com/mycommunity/viewtopic.php?p=88633*

consult your doctor about any bleeding you are having during any stage of pregnancy.

♥ **How can I find a pro-life physician in my area?**

You can call or visit a local Crisis Pregnancy Center in your area [10] and ask them for referrals to a local pro-life physician, or you can go online and visit http://www.aaplog.org/physiciansearch.aspx (American Association of Pro Life Obstetricians and Gynecologists) for a listing of pro-life physicians in your state.

♥ **If I think I am miscarrying, when should I call my doctor?**

Anytime you are bleeding during pregnancy, you should call your doctor right away. Bleeding during pregnancy isn't always a problem, but it is always better to err on the safe side and get it checked out.

♥ **How does my doctor know that I have miscarried?**

The doctor can tell that you are miscarrying (or that a miscarriage has happened recently) by checking your HCG levels, doing a pelvic exam, or by performing an ultrasound.

♥ **Can the birth control pill cause a miscarriage?**

---

[9]*Source: American Pregnancy Association*

[10]*Listing of Crisis Pregnancy Centers in your area can be found on the web at this link: http://www.pregnancycenters.org/advantage.asp*

Yes, it is possible for birth control pills to cause a miscarriage.

The pill works using three functions:

The first function causes a thickening of the mucus plug at the opening of the cervix. This is a contraceptive function, providing a barrier which prevents union of the sperm and ovum.

The second function is the suppression of ovulation. Without ovulation, there is no egg to be fertilized and therefore pregnancy cannot occur.

The third function of the pill, if the other two functions fail and a conception still occurs, is to harden the lining of the womb. This makes it an inhospitable environment to the week old embryo, so that it is unable to implant into the womb- the result being an early miscarriage.[11] (You can find this information on many birth control pill inserts although the language is usually obscure). [12]

Of course, having been on the pill is not a guarantee that you will miscarry. Many women have conceived while on the pill

---

[11]You can read more about the pill and its' effects in the book, "Does the Birth Control Pill Cause Abortions?" by Randy Alcorn. It is available online for free in PDF or HTML format at http://www.epm.com

You can also order a paperback copy for only $3.00 From Eternal Perspective Ministries: 39085 Pioneer Blvd., Suite 206, Sandy, OR 97055

[12]You can see a copy of an Ortho Tri-Cyclen® insert at this link: http://www.quiverfull.com/birth_control/CYCLTRI.PDF

and their babies have made it to term without any problems. But it is always better to err on the side of caution.

♥ Will it be painful (natural miscarriage)?

It is hard to say with certainty whether your experience will be physically painful or not, as every woman's experience is so different.

In very early miscarriages, the cramping you feel most likely will be only slightly stronger than menstrual cramps. You may not even notice a difference, depending on how early the miscarriage is.

The further along you are, the stronger the cramping is likely to be. Some women describe pain that is comparable to labor pains, but some women say that the cramping isn't any worse than their typical menstrual cramping. Some women who have had multiple miscarriages have described varied levels of pain for each miscarriage.

If you ask your doctor, she will usually be willing to prescribe you some appropriate pain medication which can help ease any pain from miscarriage.

Note: *Heavy cramping during a miscarriage is not usually a medical emergency. However, if you have any reason to suspect that you might have an ectopic pregnancy, please see a doctor to be safe.*

♥ Will it be painful (D & C)?

If you use general anesthesia or, local anesthesia with sedation, you shouldn't feel anything during the procedure. You may end up having no memory of it at all. Many women prefer this option.

If you use a local anesthesia, you may experience moderate to severe cramping during the procedure.

Afterward, you may experience nausea, vomiting, and sore throat from the general anesthesia.

You may also experience mild to moderate cramping. These symptoms should last only a few days, but can sometimes be longer. Your doctor can prescribe pain medication as needed.

♥ How long will the bleeding last (natural miscarriage)?

The first day or two of the bleeding should be the heaviest days.

The bleeding usually will last 1-2 weeks, but can sometimes last up to 4 weeks. Your doctor will be able to monitor you to ensure that your miscarriage has completed and that there are no signs of infection.

♥ How long will the bleeding last (D & C)?

Typically, bleeding should last a few days to a week after a D & C. Regular menstrual cycles should begin again in 6-8 weeks.

It is important to follow up with your doctor, so that s/he can be sure that the D & C was completed and that there are no signs of infection.

♥ When can we start trying again?

Some doctors will recommend that you wait at least 2- 3 cycles, so that your uterine lining has more time to heal and rebuild itself (also, so that it will be easier to calculate the baby's age should you become pregnant again). However, other doctors will say that you will be physically ready again after the first cycle returns. It really is up to you and when you feel emotionally and physically ready to try again.

♥ What is a Chemical Pregnancy?

A chemical pregnancy is the medical term used to describe a very early miscarriage. In a chemical pregnancy, a positive pregnancy test is seen before the woman's period was due, but a miscarriage happens before a heartbeat is detectable by ultrasound.

♥ How can you know you have had a Chemical Pregnancy?

It is actually possible to have an early miscarriage like this without even being aware of it. Because of the fact that most of these occur before the embryo has implanted in the uterus, there are sometimes no pregnancy symptoms, such as nausea, fatigue, etc. It may just seem like a late period, sometimes heavier than normal (sometimes including small blood clots). However, some women do have a pregnancy symptom, which usually leads them to take a pregnancy test earlier than normal.

A chemical pregnancy is no less of a loss than any other form of miscarriage.

♥ What is a "Missed Miscarriage"?

A missed miscarriage happens when the body does not recognize the death of an unborn child. Most of the time, the woman is unaware that her child has died until weeks after the fact.

Missed miscarriages are usually recognized when no fetal heart rate can be heard through echo-Doppler testing.

The hardest part about this type of miscarriage is the fact that it happens without warning. Pregnancy symptoms (such as morning sickness and fatigue) are still continued because pregnancy hormones are still present in the system. When the sad news is presented, it is completely unexpected. One minute, the mother is looking forward to the ultrasound of her baby…the next moment, she is told her baby has passed away.

Most missed miscarriages occur within the first 12 weeks of pregnancy. It is not always known why they happen, although the doctor can order blood tests to check for possible causes.

♥ If I am having a missed miscarriage, how long do I have to wait to miscarry naturally?

Even a few days can seem like an eternity when you are expecting to miscarry.

The length of time you have to wait really depends on the situation, as each woman's body is different.

Approximately 70 percent of women who miscarry naturally

have had a complete miscarriage within 14 days of the diagnosis. However, for some women it can take several weeks.

Your doctor will be able to keep an eye on you and make sure that things are progressing like they should.

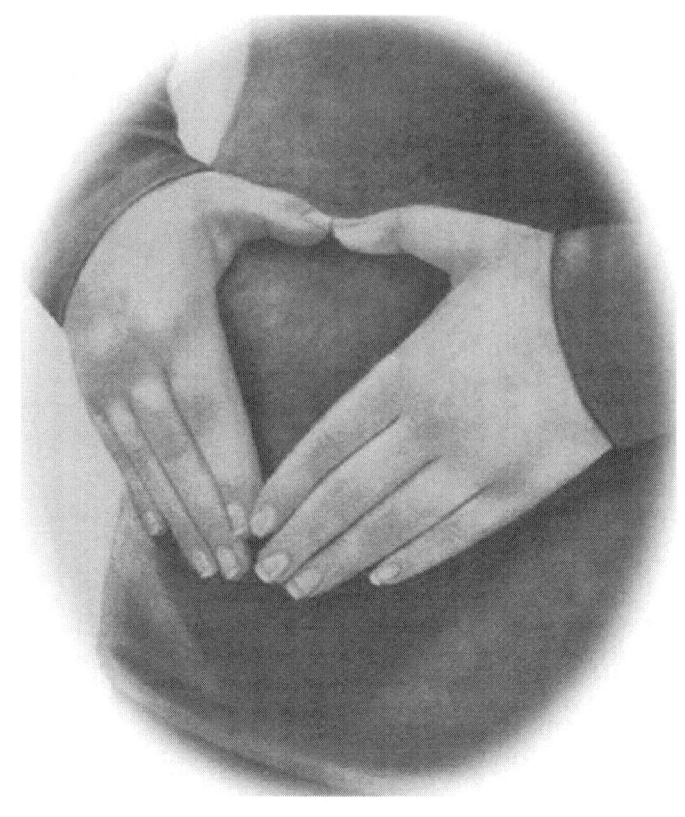

Stories about Miscarriage

Sara's Story

"I had a beautiful daughter and when she was 17 months old, I found out I was pregnant with my second child. My husband and I weren't trying to have any babies, but I was late on my period and I figured I should test- and sure enough, when I took the test, it was positive.

It took awhile for it to sink in; I was in shock. I was really happy, and scared at the same time, because I never would have dreamed that I would have children this close together.

Being a worry wart, I made an appointment with the doctor so I could confirm that I was pregnant. After being confirmed, I began to accept the fact that in 9 months I would be holding another precious baby in my arms.

Everything seemed fine at first. I was feeling good, and a couple of weeks passed. By that time I was fine with the idea of having this baby and actually excited to be pregnant again!

On the morning of Feb. 13, I was about to leave with my mom for a hair appointment. As I was getting ready, I started to realize something didn't feel right. I continued to get ready, and right before I left, I told my mom that I needed to use the restroom.

When I went to the bathroom, the nightmare began- I was spotting. I automatically began crying, and at this point I just knew I was losing the baby. I told my mother that she could go on, and that I was going to stay and call the doctor, to try to get an appointment that day. I couldn't get in until that afternoon- the waiting was horrible.

The contractions started, and I was in so much pain, but I didn't want to take anything, just in case the baby was still thriving. I went from spotting to passing lots of blood. I sat and cried and cried.

Finally, it was time to go to the doctor. My husband, John, was able to go with me, and my mother watched my daughter. The doctor said that I was probably losing the baby, but that they would take some blood tests, and the next week I would be able to know whether I had truly lost the baby.

When I was in the doctor's waiting room, I had to run to the bathroom, and that is when I knew for sure that I had lost the baby, because of all of the clots I lost.

I remember lying in the doctor's room, crying, and just wishing someone would pinch me and wake me from this horrible nightmare. I yearned to hold my daughter, knowing that I could be confident she was with me and not leaving me like the one that went to Heaven.

It was the saddest moment of my life.

Realizing that I would not get to hold this baby, and kiss this baby; that I would not be able to watch him/her grow up and celebrate birthdays was too much for me to handle. I went home and cried and held my daughter, and began telling all of my family the sad news. I also began to take some pain relievers because of the pain I was in. I was in a state of shock. I went from waiting patiently to meet my baby, to losing the baby, in an instant.

Many people told me, "It wasn't meant to be", or "It wasn't very far along"...those words really hurt, even though I know they didn't mean it that way. I didn't *care* if I wasn't that far along, and I didn't *care* if it was meant to be! I just had a life taken from me; one that was beginning to grow, and I was waiting to meet him/her.

I didn't like going places and seeing babies anymore. When I found out that my sister-in-law was expecting, it tore me apart. I didn't hate her for it; I just wanted my baby back.

I strongly believe that I have a baby in heaven, and for some odd reason, I think the baby was a boy. I think my baby boy is with my Grandpa McConnell in Heaven. He was due on Oct. 13. Every time that Oct. 13 comes around, I think of how old he would be then. I will never forget my baby that is in Heaven now. I miss him and love him very much."

Penny's Story

"When our only child was only 21 months, I was hemorrhaging and was told that if I didn't have a D&C, I would die. This puts a Christian in a very difficult position. Truly I was hemorrhaging and in great distress physically and emotionally. My first pregnancy was so easy and the birth and delivery went without a hitch. My doctor was a Christian and I relied heavily on her understanding of my belief that abortion is wrong. She told me I had no other choice and considering the amount of blood loss and the buzzing of the machines around me in the emergency room, I believe in my heart that this is true. There was no heart beat found at this time and I was told the usual, "It was never a viable pregnancy"? These words haunted me for so long. When did it become a "non-viable" pregnancy? I knew something was different. I was growing differently than my 1st pregnancy and had mentioned to my sister that something seemed very different.

When my husband took me to the emergency room that night, it had been snowing. It was just after midnight on St Patrick's Day. I was scared as I'd never experienced the amount of blood loss and the feeling of what was coming out of me - frightening! I just cried and cried, wrapped twice in a blanket from my waist down to keep the car clean. It was soaked within the 15 minutes it took to get to the hospital. The snow seemed so perfect.

When I was discharged the next morning, my husband pushed me out of the hospital in the wheel chair. I felt overwhelmed with sadness as we all know a mother with her new baby is pushed out in the same wheelchair, and here I was, with empty arms.

When we got outside, I was overwhelmed by the brightest sunny day one could expect in rainy Oregon in March! At that moment, I felt God had replaced that snowy night with a sunny day to give me peace. I was so happy! Truly happy! Only God can bring that peace in your life.

I was rocking our daughter that night, before putting her to bed. I'm sure you remember just wanting to hold your children close for comfort? The rocking chair was in the corner of her bedroom with a window behind us. I was rocking and humming to her and she kept looking over my head and smiling, as if someone was there. I turned around at one point to see what she was looking at, and of course saw nothing. I closed my eyes and suddenly heard her say, "Mommy, Jesus loves you". 21 months old, with an excellent vocabulary, this still surprised me! I said, "What?" She said, "Jesus loves you". WOW! I don't know what God allowed her to "see". An angel? The baby? Himself?

I do know that her message came right from the mouth of God. I'll never forget these 2 signs of His love and comfort at such a low point in my life. I will never be the same person I was before the miscarriage, but thank God for what He gave me to get through my darkest days."

Amanda's Story

On August 17, 2009 my alarm went off and I got up to get ready for work. I stood before the bathroom sink for a moment, and then sat down to use the bathroom. I felt a large 'something' between my legs... I said 'oh no' out loud, but mostly to myself because I was certain that what I was feeling was a large blood clot. I put my hand down to see if it was blood, and instead, I caught my tiny baby; my tiny, precious, perfect (although small) baby.

I called to my husband, Matt, and we held our baby and cried.

On the way to the ER we decided we would have a funeral and that no matter what...we were going to leave the hospital with our baby and not leave it there to be 'dealt with.' The nurses in the triage area wanted to take the baby and when they pulled out the 'specimen' bag I nearly fainted. We had the baby in a Tupperware container, and I clutched it to my chest. I told the nurse there was no way I was leaving the hospital without my baby. My OBGYN was called and they sent me to a room to wait for her arrival. After I was checked-out by my regular doctor, it was decided I would need a D&C, as I hadn't bled at all. I had no contractions and no pain...but, I had my tiny baby 26 weeks early.

While waiting my turn for surgery (nearly 12 hours) I developed an infection. My fever was high before the D&C and did not come down until 3 days later. I sent my husband home with the baby, and a temporary plan to hold a small funeral sometime later that week. We knew that we wanted to name the baby, but none of the names we had talked of before our loss seemed appropriate. So, my husband went searching for the perfect name, but nothing seemed right. And then one day he came to the hospital and had a few names written on a scrap of paper...and among them was the name Rowan. It means simply 'little red one.' Our tiny love was so small, and so red. The name perfectly captured our hearts. Rowan McCleskey, our Glory Baby...perfect.

We cannot comprehend the hopelessness of losing a child and not knowing Christ. Therefore, we started *Rowan's Hope* (now titled *"This Girl Will Never be the Same")*, http://thisgirl-amanda.blogspot.com/, to be a place of education and hope for women and families who have lost a child to miscarriage.

In addition I have found great healing in writing my blog. There are so many women who write about their loss, and I have found courage in their words. I have wept with them, rejoiced with them and prayed for them. I certainly hope that is what people are doing when they read my blog.

Rebecca's Story

I had been going out with my boyfriend for a few months and we were getting along great. When I was late for my period, I didn't imagine I could be pregnant as I had always been "careful".

I passed a pharmacy after a few days and thought I might as well check, not for one minute expecting the test to be positive. I hadn't told a soul, and I took the test alone. When I saw the two lines, I thought I was seeing things, so I took a picture on my phone and said I'd look at the photo later and see if it was still there.

I went off and met up with friends that afternoon and didn't mention anything. That night I looked at the photo and it sunk in that I really was pregnant. I was terrified but so happy. My best friend figured it out in 24 hours without me saying a word and I confessed to her that I was pregnant. I knew immediately I would keep my baby (nothing else was ever an option, and although I wondered how I would manage, I knew I'd find a way).

When I told my boyfriend, he asked me to get an abortion. It hurt me so very much that he would say that, and I told him it wasn't an option and wouldn't consider it for a second. He was supportive at first, saying he'd come to my appointments with me. About a week later, he claimed I was lying and that this couldn't be his baby (that was probably the most hurtful thing anyone has ever said to me).

I told him he could have a DNA test if he wanted, as there was no chance whatsoever that this baby wasn't his. I told him that his suggesting that it wasn't his baby was cruel. He dumped me, changed his number, and the code to his apartment block so I had no way to contact him (his parents lived overseas and I didn't have their contact details).

It stung and I was in pieces. I told my mother and although she was very shocked, she was very supportive. She told the rest of the family for me and they were all so kind. They kept saying that of all the people they knew, they never imagined it would be me that would end up in this situation. I'm a good student... I do charity work in my spare time... and I'm just not the type of girl who gives her heart away easily.

The fact that I was soon going to be a single teen mom shocked them as much as it did me.

I ended up leaving my plans for college until the next year when I planned to return after my baby was born. I took up evening courses and prepared my life in every way I could. I ate healthy and took my Folic acid and vitamins religiously.

While my friends went out and partied I delighted in staying and crocheting baby blankets and searching online for the perfect baby stroller.

I thought all about how rewarding life as a mother would be. I have young nieces and nephews and knew that they could be so very demanding, but ultimately that they were a blessing.

I remember crying one night and my mum asked me why I was so upset and I told her it was because I couldn't decide what preschool was best and what if I made the wrong decision. She hugged me and told me to stop worrying and that I would be a great mom.

I made lists of names and just threw myself into learning how to be the perfect mother. I never once missed the life I'd had before and I'm sure my friends often wondered how I could literally change my entire life around virtually overnight.

I played songs to my tummy and rubbed it constantly so excited about all the joy that lay ahead. I worked hard to become healthier than I'd ever been in my life and my doctor even noted this at one appointment.

I worried constantly about miscarriage though and about whether they would be OK. It was extremely hard not to worry. The day I reached twelve weeks I breathed such a sigh of relief knowing that the chances of miscarriage at that point were slim. I stayed up late reading my pregnancy books and waiting for the day I held the baby in my arms.

My first scan was scheduled for 14 weeks and I was so excited that I could barely sleep. That morning I woke and rubbed my tummy smiling. My mum and a friend came with me. They were both beside themselves with excitement and kept asking how many copies of photos we would get so they could all have a few and show everyone.

I remember that day so vividly, it was finally my turn and I got up on the table with them at my side smiling from ear to ear. She poured the gel on my tummy and started to move the ultrasound wand around. I watched the big screen in front of me desperate to catch a glimpse of my precious little child.

The first thing that hit me was the earth shattering silence, then the nurses face as she called in another nurse. I looked at my mother while trying not to cry. She squeezed my hand and tried to smile and reassure me. I knew it was over.

The other nurse came in and tried the wand again; I looked at the screen and saw a big and deathly still blob. She turned to me with the saddest eyes I've ever seen and said "I'm so sorry Rebecca, but your baby has passed away. All that we can find is a gestational sac measuring 8 weeks and 1 day. It's likely your baby has been gone for a while now."

I literally jumped off the table and ran, collapsing in the hall and crying my eyes out. I felt like I was unable to breathe and my heart felt like it was bursting out of my chest. I hadn't had any cramping or even spotting and I'd had my last checkup two weeks before. I didn't understand how this could happen. I had done everything right! How could my baby have died and I didn't even notice?

My mother was trying not to cry as she came out with an appointment for 3 days later. She practically carried me out of the hospital. As she did, we passed a group of woman with big bumps, puffing away on cigarettes. I felt such intense anger towards them that it scared me.

She drove me to the General Practitioner so I could have some questions answered and he coldly told me "I don't know what you expect me to do about it."

I told my mom I couldn't cope with this and that she had to drive me to the mental hospital, as I felt I wouldn't be able to live at that moment and wanted to just die and be with my baby. The hospital told her I needed an appointment and we waited there for three hours as I cried hysterically, and the nurses phoned doctors demanding I be seen.

Eventually we gave up and as we drove home. The hospital rang and asked her to bring me back in saying I obviously needed to be seen but should have expected the wait without an appointment. My mother lost it when she heard that. I've never seen her so angry or upset. She asked him how I was supposed to know in advance this would happen and make an appointment. She asked them why nobody cared that I was suicidal and needed urgent attention. She got into a huge argument with him before bursting into tears and hanging up.

We decided we wouldn't go back as they were so cold and unhelpful. For the next 3 days I sat numb unable to eat or think while my sister and mother took turns looking after me.

I returned to the hospital and sat in the same waiting room as before, surrounded by happy couples fawning over their scan pictures. I cried my eyes out. My mum asked them to please get me out of there soon and I was brought in next. Another scan, and yet another shattering emptiness. I was taken to fetal assessment and told my options.

They said a natural miscarriage was unlikely for me at this point, as there had been no signs of anything happening, but that I could wait it out if I wanted. They offered to give me tablets to help start the process, and pain relief, but also said that 4 out of 10 women failed to respond to the treatment. The last option was surgical, a D&C, the doctor explained I would be admitted to hospital and have "products" removed. It infuriated me that they used that word.

I went home and looked up every single bit of information on each that I could find, weighing the pros and cons of each trying to decide what was best. I opted for the D & C, as I felt I

couldn't wait another second with my poor baby not
being alive but still being inside me. The idea that I could take
the tablets and being in pain while still having the possibility of
a D&C looming was too much and I didn't believe I could
emotionally cope with any of it. I asked them about the
statistics for the hospital in relation to *Ashermans syndrome*
and if it could affect my chances of conceiving in the future in
any way. They said there hadn't been a case in the hospital
since it opened and not a case in the whole country since the
60s.

The day I went for the D & C, I stayed awake all night before,
in the hope that I would sleep through as much of the day as I
could. At 5:00, I took the tablets they had given me, and
shortly afterward, I began having cramps and mild bleeding.
Thankfully I slept through most of this due to sheer exhaustion
and was admitted to hospital at 7am.

Once I got there i went to sleep again and was awakened to be
taken to surgery after an hour. The minute I put the gown on I
became hysterical and cried my eyes out. The nurse was kind
and asked me about my baby. I waited outside the room to go
in and cried as I looked through my medical file staring at
the scan pictures I never got and that terrible emptiness. I was
hysterical. There was 3 nurses trying to calm me down but I
just couldn't stop crying and I was so scared. One nurse held
my hand and next thing I knew I was in the recovery room.
The minute I opened my eyes the tears started all over again. I
was taken to my room and slept for several hours.

When I woke up I felt a little better and was given tea and
a little memory book to remember the little life that had
changed mine. I went home at 5pm tired and feeling like I'd

done a few rounds in a boxing ring.

Over the coming days I took painkillers every 4 hours like clockwork but still had stomach pains. I worried I was imagining it as the bleeding wasn't bad.7 days later I thought the bleeding had stopped and although the cramps were still bad enough to make me keep taking painkillers I thought I was through it. That night I started having waves of intense pain in my stomach. It scared me a lot and I knew something was wrong. They came in waves. After reading others accounts of a natural miscarriage online and about how it felt like contractions, I knew the doctor had missed something. I ended up spending the night in complete agony as it was two in the morning and I knew what was happening. I decided to go to the doctors first thing in the morning. I passed very large clots and it was very painful.

Eventually I passed out from the pain, and when I woke the next day the pain was gone. I went to my doctor afraid it would happen again and looking for answers. He felt my stomach and actually listened to it with a stethoscope (which made me upset as I kept thinking, Oh no, is he hearing a heartbeat? Have I just killed my baby? This was just a fleeting thought and I soon calmed down after I reminded myself that I had seen the proof myself in the notes, and I was fooling myself to think like that).

He sent me straight to the emergency department of the maternity hospital. After spending the day in a bed on the emergency room with the loud galloping sound of the heartbeats of the babies being monitored on either side of me as their mothers waited to be transferred to the labor room, I felt like my brain was melting (It was so loud and they were surrounding me).

I had to have an internal scan and again I cried. This time all that I saw was white shapes. The nurse was very good and scanned my ovaries as well and told me that everything pointed to a healthy reproductive system, that there was no signs of damage, and that I should be able to conceive in the future with no problems.

I was told I had fluid in the uterus and an infection and given antibiotics. Thankfully they did the trick and I began to feel physically myself again soon after.

Ectopic Loss Stories

Rheanon's Story

November 29th was a great day because it was the day I found out I was pregnant. I was a little shocked being that I was expecting ovulation, and not pregnancy. After five days of positive ovulation results, I finally decided to take a pregnancy test. It was POSITIVE!!! I went to the clinic and got a blood test done and it was positive. At that point I had no idea how far along I was. I either ovulated right after my period or was about three weeks along, or I conceived at the end of Oct., had a period, and was about seven to eight weeks along. A quantitative HCG the next day determined that I was the latter.

All along, though, something didn't feel right about this pregnancy because of how everything happened as explained above. I was so nervous and paranoid that something was wrong, but everyone kept insisting that everything was okay. I tried to go along with it as much as I could, and I tried to be happy about it, but I still had this daunting feeling about it.

Then, on Dec. 9th I had horrible cramping that night, and while I know that menstrual-type cramping is normal during pregnancy, this wasn't the norm.

The next day I told my husband that I needed to go to the clinic because I was concerned. I went in and they had me do some lab work, a physical, & then finally the ultrasound. I was praying so hard before they came to do the ultrasound. I prayed to God and asked him to show me the baby.

I wanted to see that baby on the screen, even if they dropped the horrible news that I was going to miscarry. They finally performed the ultrasound and there was NOTHING! There was no gestational sac, and my uterine lining wasn't even thick enough to support a pregnancy. After getting a positive pregnancy test, after experiencing all of the early pregnancy symptoms, and after expecting an August 2008 baby they told me there was no baby in my uterus. "NO!!?" I wondered, "How could that be???"

They sent me to Radiology to get several more ultrasounds done, so they could check for an ectopic pregnancy. The results from that was NO BABY! My OB told me that they didn't find a baby in my tubes or uterus, but they still weren't ruling out an ectopic. His diagnosis was to do a D&C and give me the drug, "Methotrexate" to terminate the supposed "pregnancy". I say "supposed" because at that point I felt so empty and cheated because there was no baby. I felt like I had some rare medical condition where I produced HCG for no reason. I felt like a failure!

I declined the D&C for the simple fact that there was nothing in my uterus and I didn't want them scraping around in there for no reason. Not to mention my dates could have been wrong and I thought maybe I wasn't far enough long for them to see a baby. The OB asked me to come back in 24 hours to do an HCG to see what my levels were going to do. Right before I got the call for my results, I had this slim ray of hope that maybe my theory was right. Well, the results came and in 24 hours my HCG only went up six, so we knew at that point that there wasn't going to be a viable pregnancy. I still felt confused and empty because I never saw a baby. I told the OB that if I was going to miscarry that my body could do it on its own and I didn't need a D&C for that purpose. I came back 24 hours later and did another HCG test, but never got a call from my OB as to what was going on with my levels. That was pretty much going to determine if it was ectopic or miscarriage. This was on a Friday and I just assumed that everything was okay, and I decided that I would call the OB on the following Monday.

Well the next day, Dec. 15th, I was freaking out because the National Weather warnings kept saying we were under a tornado warning. I called my husband, Blake, at work to see if he knew anymore than I did and he told me that he would call me back. A few minutes before he called back I started getting these pains in my lower abdomen. He called back and could tell something was wrong. He asked me if I was okay and I told him that I had some mild pain in my stomach. I lay on the floor, thinking that it would make it go away, but it didn't and the pain kept getting much worse.

Blake started getting worried and asked me if I wanted him to come home. I didn't know what to do at first because I didn't want him to come home and my pains be nothing. I waited for a few more minutes and as the pain got worse I told him to go ahead and come home.

When he was on his way home, my pain got so bad that if I tried to move it was excruciating. I called him and he told me to call the ambulance, but he ended up doing it for me. He got home just in time as they arrived. They loaded me up on the stretcher and away we went. Blake stayed home because Abby (my daughter) was still napping. I told him to just come to the E.R. when she woke up. At this point, I knew it was ectopic because I had the symptoms, but I certainly didn't realize the extent of my situation. '

When I got to the ER, they took my blood pressure and hooked me to an IV. They continued to monitor my blood pressure and at some point it just started plummeting. My room started getting crowded with people and they put an IV in my other arm. One of the nurses asked me if I had anybody at the hospital with me and I told her no. She told me that someone should be there and I told her why my hubby was still home, so she called Blake for me to tell him to come as soon as possible. He was pulling in the ER as she called. He told me that when he came in they let him know that my blood pressure was starting to get very low.

Both he and Abby came into my room, and I felt such relief to see those two faces. I could tell Blake was a little upset and I felt bad. The crazy thing is that this whole time I never realized how critical my situation was. I remember laying there wanting to hold Abby and talk to her, but I had no strength to do anything. Blake said my face was jaundiced. I'm really surprised that I didn't pass out or throw up everywhere.

At its lowest, my blood pressure went down to 77 over 38. God was definitely present, keeping me sane and calm.

My OB finally showed up and told us that my tube had ruptured and that I was bleeding internally. He said that I would have to have surgery to remove my tube and, of course, he had to tell me all of the worse case scenarios, which were removal of both tubes, ovaries, & my uterus. When he left the room, I looked at Blake and started to freak out. Blake said, "Don't worry; he just has to tell you all of the possibilities!!" At that point, I was more worried about losing my God-given privilege of child bearing than losing my own life!

I probably sat in the ER for a good hour or so before they finally took me up for surgery. Blake was fuming because I was laying there hemorrhaging internally and in the meantime they are waiting on the surgical nurse to show up. I could feel my stomach filling up with blood because it felt very bloated and cold. It was a very strange feeling.

Finally, all of the right people showed up and my surgery was performed. Blake went home in the meantime, but came back up there when I came out of surgery. My OB briefed him on the surgery and told him to go home as I would probably sleep for the rest of the night because of the anesthesia and pain medication. Not to mention, it was late and Abby was ready for bed. I ended up waking up and kept asking my nurse where Blake was. She thought he was still there, so she went looking for him. She came back and told me that he wasn't there, so I called him and he was at home. I felt so alone and I just burst into tears because the one thing I wanted was for him and Abby to be there with me. He felt so awful and offered to wake Abby up to come up there, but I told him not to and that I would get over it somehow. I felt like this was one of the saddest moments in my life. I was completely and utterly alone! With my husband being in the Air Force we live far from home, so we have no family or friends where we live to help us out.

My original OB had told Blake that he wanted him to be off for a week, but he didn't give Blake any documents stating anything about the leave. My doctor went on emergency leave the next morning (the night after my surgery).

Another OB took over my case and I asked her about recommending leave for Blake. She told me that she doesn't give a week off for her c-section patients and that they go home and take care of their kids just fine, so I shouldn't need him at home to take care of me. She said that she would give him a day or two and that was it. Can it get more unsympathetic than that?? This lady couldn't even take into consideration what I had just gone through. I didn't go through a c-section where the end result is a sweet baby! I had gone through losing a part of my reproductive system where the end result might be even MORE difficulty in having another baby! (Not to mention, I had lost a lot of blood which required two blood transfusions and could barely lift myself out of bed, let alone lifting a toddler). Nevertheless, my husband ended up getting the leave, but I was furious that I had to deal with this after going through a tragic situation.

On top of all of this, I really wanted my mom to be here by my side. I felt like she was insensitive to my situation in so many ways. She definitely could have found the time to be here with me as I needed her the most. When I first found out about the ectopic she told me that I couldn't continue to do this to myself. I'm 26-years-old and she tried telling me after only having one child that I should stop trying for another baby. She said that a person can only handle so much grief before they have a mental breakdown. OUCH!!! Not the right thing to say in my situation. Then after my surgery, she tells me that I need to fly back home in the next couple of days because it would be more convenient for her to take care of me. WHAT? Flying a few days after my surgery, after losing 1/3 of my blood, with a two-year-old is NOT possible. I could barely take care of myself let alone my daughter.

She was just very insensitive on all levels and it was too much to swallow! I was very upset and angry with her for about a week, but because God commands us to forgive I did. It still hurts to think that my mom couldn't figure out a way to be here for me, but life goes on, right??

Emotionally, I was a wreck for the first few days. I mostly reflected on how critical my situation was and of course losing one of my tubes. I keep forgetting that I only have one tube, so when I remember I only have one I get upset. I still get emotional when I think about not having a baby in my arms this summer. It really hurts that I have the hardest time carrying a pregnancy. But above all, I still have a lot of faith that God will bless us again, but I know I will be a nervous wreck when it happens. I hope that my story will help those ladies out there that have experienced an ectopic pregnancy or a loss of any kind. May God bless us abundantly when His Will bids it!

Heather's Story

I didn't even know that I was pregnant. I should have suspected that I was. All my other 4 pregnancies had been conceived around the same time of year to give me late fall and early winter babies. It was my normal time to get pregnant. But I didn't connect the tiredness with pregnancy. You see, I still was getting what I thought was my period each month.

It was the end of May 2006, the 23rd to be exact. I was busy with the 4 boys and didn't give the tiredness any thought. That is, until I started with mid-cycle bleeding. I was just spotting at first. Then the pain started. Not bad in the beginning. I didn't know who to call about it. My regular OB/GYN office had just closed down at the beginning of the month. I figured I had just overdone it and that's why I was hurting and that the spotting was related to ovulating. Popped a few ibuprofen and went on with my day.

As the day progressed, I got a bit more uncomfortable. It was bedtime, and I had complained of the pain to my husband, but still didn't think much of it. However, I had this nagging feeling in the back of my mind. As the night wore on, I couldn't get any sleep as the pain was getting worse. I snuck downstairs to go online for awhile and for some reason found myself typing Ectopic pregnancy into the search engine. I sat there reading the symptoms and realized that there might be a connection with them and what I was feeling. Day dawned and I told Leo, my husband, that I was going to call our regular doctor and go from there. I still hadn't let Leo know what I thought might be wrong. He left for work and I began my day:

Normal stuff; housework taking care of the kids, etc. I called our doctor, and I guess I kind of downplayed my symptoms too much. Didn't want them to think I was a complainer. They said they'd call if they had an opening. Not what I wanted to hear, but I said OK.

So I went about my business at home. I felt as if all the energy was draining out of me. Five ibuprofens didn't even touch the pain. The spotting had become a little heavier but still not as much as a period. Leo called and asked me how I was doing. I told him and he decided to call the doctor's office back for me. In fact, he decided to circumvent the front desk and talked to one of our friends that was a nurse at the office and got me in for a 6 PM appointment. When he called back, I started getting the diaper bags, etc together so that I'd be ready to go when he got home. Even tossed in some stuff for me-an embroidery project that I was working on at the time, figured I'd do that while he drove since we had a 1/2 hour drive to the doctors.

We get to the office and Leo waits in the truck with the four boys while I go in. Since it is evening hours for appointments, it really wasn't too busy. I go in the back and wait in the exam room. When the doctor comes in, I tell him my symptoms. He pokes my back a bit, and my stomach, and tells me it could likely be one of two things: a kidney infection or an Ectopic pregnancy. I got chills when he said that. He told me to go leave a sample in the bathroom and they would do a pregnancy test when I was done. Since he knew that we hadn't been using anything for birth control, he said to me "And after this is all over with, maybe you should come back in and we will talk about using birth control". I wasn't too happy with him, but headed to the bathroom to leave my deposit. Back to the exam room I go, sitting there by myself wondering what is going on with my body.

The doctor comes back in, and tells me that the test was positive and that he wanted me to go over to the ER and be seen that night, ASAP. I told him I had to drop off my kids with the grandparents and then I would head over.

As I walked out to the truck, I was shaking and crying. Leo saw how pale I was and noticed I was shaking. He asked me what was wrong and I told him. During the short drive to his parents' house I tried to make sense of what was going on. Leo didn't really say much or maybe I just can't remember any conversation. I was in shock.

We pulled in the driveway at Leo's parents' house, and his mom met us at the door. I told her what was going on, and it was quickly decided by everyone that my mother in law would drive me to the hospital so that Leo could stay home with the boys. You see, our youngest was 1 1/2 and needed one of his parents with him. In retrospect, I wish I had kept my husband and my baby with me. It was the first night I'd been away from Caleb, and it wasn't a comfortable night since he was still nursing.

We arrived at the hospital ER. And so the wait began. Later I was told that because I wasn't presenting as a "classic" Ectopic pregnancy (severe pain, etc) I was not given high priority when in the waiting area. Guess in times like that it doesn't pay to have a high tolerance for pain. Once in the back, I got asked the million and one questions about my sex life, etc, in front of my mother in law. In between nurses questioning me, I thought to apologize for having her come to the hospital on her birthday. She said it was definitely a birthday she wouldn't forget. I got to meet the on call OB/GYN. She treated me with respect and kindness, and that's why I switched to her office on the spot. I was sent for an US, and the tech really didn't want to say much as to what she was seeing on the screen. I think I saw my baby, but I'm not sure. I went back to the ER exam room. Blood draws left and right. My doctor comes in and asks me what I'd like to do. She wasn't 100% sure it was Ectopic. Tests leaned in that direction though. Did I want to do the surgery immediately or have them observe me over night? I decided to be observed.

Meanwhile, Leo came over after Caleb had gone to sleep. He didn't stay long, but I sent my rings and purse home with him when he left with his mom. Leo wasn't too talkative, and very tired from working all day in the hot machine shop, so I told him to leave. I also thought it would be better if he was with Caleb should he wake up and need me.

I get transferred to my room on the maternity floor. It was right across from the newborn nursery. I don't think they were thinking when they put me in there. The nurses on that floor, as always where very nice. When you are a frequent visitor, they remember you. Lots of blood draws, lots of encouraging and comforting words. They offered me pain medication. Sleep was fleeting, and as May 25th arrived, I was in conversation with my new doctor. Tests were leaning even more towards Ectopic. It was decided that we would do the surgery laparoscopically, and if all was normal, she'd leave me pregnant and all would be great.

I was in the hospital near the OR where the surgery is to be done. I had another long wait. Since I was not feeling any pain at the moment due to the pain medications, I was sitting up and flipping through my chart that had info from my other visits to the maternity ward. Very interesting reading! That is, until the pain started coming back. By the time I was wheeled into the OR, I was curled in a ball in pain, praying that my baby was going to be OK, and that it was in the right place. And praying that if it wasn't that my baby could forgive me for ending its life if it was still alive (that was something I don't know, and really don't want to know-was my baby alive when the surgery began). I was talking to my baby and holding my hand to my stomach to hold the baby.

Into the Operating Room I was pushed. Everyone, myself included, had a brief laugh since I still had my bra on and we had to take it off over the IV pole lines before they settled me on the table. Last thing I remembered was that and the blue walls and many cabinets in that room before my IV line was injected with something to put me out.

I woke up in recovery wrapped in heated blankets. I fell back asleep. I don't remember much between there and going back to my room on the maternity floor. Guess what, that was considered outpatient surgery! I was sent home that afternoon, and I could barely walk. The pain was tremendous. I couldn't even zip my pants due to the gauze pads over my 3 small incisions. I knew I'd lost my baby and that hurt horribly.

I was 8 to 9 weeks along and my left tube had ruptured. They saved the tube, but not my baby. I regret not asking for my baby's remains so that I could bury them.

Leo was waiting in my room when I was wheeled up. We gathered my stuff and headed to pick up the kids to go home. While no one told me I had to, I just pushed myself to continue with life as usual. No one had any groups to go talk to about ectopic pregnancy loss. I found groups for miscarriage, but not ectopic pregnancy. I ended up finding a group online to talk to. Leo and I didn't talk much about what had happened. One family member was so callous as to say "why didn't you get your tubes tied while they had you open already?" Others said things to the affect that I should be happy with the 4 healthy boys I had.

Here I was walking bent over with incisions that hurt like mad, and I was expected to carry on as usual. We did cancel our camping trip for that weekend, but we still had to go visit the in laws down there anyway. Each bump in the road was renewed agony, and getting out of the truck was not much fun.

Time has passed, but we still don't talk about what happened much. I have tried to work through my grief. I named my baby Morgan because that is the name that was whispered in my heart by God. I don't know if Morgan is a girl or a boy, but I will see my child some day in Heaven. For now, Morgan gets to play at Gods feet.

I miss my baby so much, and have a load of guilt I bear. You see, 3 months after I lost Morgan, I became pregnant with my daughter Tammy. As that pregnancy progressed normally, and my scars from the surgery stretched with her growth, I was reminded of my loss. Tammy's due date was May 30th, five days after the anniversary of Morgan's surgery. As late December/early January came and went, so passed the time when I should have been welcoming Morgan into my arms. But if I had Morgan, I wouldn't have Tammy. I feel guilt for wanting both, but knowing that one would have had to die or never be conceived for the other to live. Tammy was born on May 16, 2007. I induced labor due to gestational diabetes. It was good to have her in my arms that ached for a baby, but having her didn't make me forget the anniversary of losing Morgan.

Here I sit, 3 years almost to the day later since losing Morgan. Each time I have back pain, I fear it's happening again. When I get pregnant, I have to notify the OB office as soon as I test positive so we can get an ultrasound done to make sure that the baby is in the right place. I had an ultrasound at 5 weeks gestation with Tammy, just as our family was mourning the death of Leo's sister, whom he decided to honor by naming our daughter after her.

Have I fully grieved the loss of my baby? No. Have I found healing and comfort since my loss? I have found some, but not completely. I can only hope that I will find the comfort and healing that I need. Has my marriage suffered because of this? Yes, it has. I felt deserted in the hospital by my husband. I felt he was not even on the same wave length as me. I wanted him to acknowledge our baby, to talk about what happened. I don't even know if he knows I've named the baby Morgan. Will we ever recover as a couple from this? I really don't know.

When people ask me how many children I have, I say 5, but my heart screams out 6. I have a birthstone necklace that I'm replacing the hanging charms with one for each child, including one for Morgan. The living children will be represented by gold with the birthstones set in it. Morgan will have a silver and emerald charm.

And so I close this story of the impact that a tiny life that I only knew of its existence for a few short hours. Those hours left a deep mark on me; both on the inside on my soul, and on the outside with my 3 little scars that are a reminder each time I shower or change my clothes.

"I really haven't found complete comfort and peace since the loss. It hasn't helped to have lots of upheaval in your life during the 3 yrs since, but I'll tell you something. Telling you about what happened to me helps a little. People glaze over when you start to talk about an ectopic pregnancy. They really do. No one offers to cook you a meal, no flowers, no sympathy cards. It's business as usual. Back to the daily grind, just bury the feelings and never let them show because you might upset others. We who have lost a baby that was ectopic want to talk it out. We just need someone to listen. "

Jan's Story

My husband and I married in 1995 and knew almost immediately that we wanted to start a family. When I didn't conceive within a few months I knew something was wrong. I was only 21 at the time and had always been perfectly healthy. Most of the women in my family had been able to have numerous children, so when I didn't get pregnant within six months, I instinctively knew something wasn't right.

Before our first anniversary, I scheduled an appointment with my OB/GYN and that started us on a path of numerous tests and treatments. This went on for seven years. Nothing worked and eventually I had to have an ovary removed due to endometriosis.

In 2002 we decided to adopt and began the process of becoming certified foster parents so that we could adopt through the foster system. In mid-2003 we brought home two sibling groups within weeks of one another. Inside of a month, we had an instant family of two boys and two girls.

A few months later, just after my 30th birthday, I discovered that I was pregnant. We knew immediately that something was wrong because I didn't even realize I was pregnant until I began spotting at the wrong time of the month. I took a pregnancy test just to rule that out, not really thinking I was pregnant. It was positive. We were ecstatic, but worried at the same time ,because this was not in any way normal spotting.

I called my doctor and she had me come in that afternoon. After confirming I was pregnant, she ordered blood tests and discovered that my hormone levels were not very high. For the next two weeks, she had blood tests performed every other day in the hopes that the hormone levels would begin to increase as they needed to. It never happened.

She performed an ultrasound and couldn't see anything in the womb. She also couldn't see anything else, however, and I was not having any other problems other than the spotting. She informed us that the pregnancy would most likely end in miscarriage.

So, we began to wait for the inevitable, all the while praying for a miracle. Another week passed and still nothing. My doctor wanted to perform another ultrasound. She still could not see the baby but was concerned that I had a specific type of ectopic pregnancy. Due to the fact that we live an hour from the hospital, she admitted me for observation.

20 minutes later, my tube burst and I had to have emergency surgery. The tube in which the baby had embedded was on the right side and I had already lost my ovary on the left side, which meant that I was left with one tube and one ovary on opposite sides of one another. This makes it almost impossible to pregnant again.

When I was released from the hospital, the only thing I wanted to do was get back to my life with my husband and our four children whom we were still in the process of adopting. My doctor warned me that I might experience some postpartum depression, but I just waved it off and tried to get back to my life. Within a month I knew she was very much correct. Because I lost the baby when I was only 9 weeks, I had not understood that postpartum depression would be something to be concerned about. Yet, it was very much a problem. That, along with the grief over losing the baby and knowing that I would probably never be able to get pregnant again, was very difficult. I also was not prepared for the way that one experience would change me. I'm not sure how to explain it, but it definitely changed me.

At the time I managed a state employment office. That was a very stressful and time intensive job. I lost the baby in early April and by the end of May my supervisors were pressuring me to work more and more. I was already working 40 or more hours and I just suddenly stepped back and looked at the situation and thought to myself, *"You know, this just isn't working. I'm not adopting these children to have daycare raise them."* So, I quit my job within the week and came home with the faith that it would all work it. At the time, I couldn't have possibly known what God had in store for us.

For a while, we had considered opening a daycare at our home. We worked toward achieving that goal, but found out that we would not be able to do this because the children were still technically in foster care. This seemed like a setback but I was confident that something else would work out. Fall was approaching by this time and I was not particularly looking forward to the end of November. I had lost my mother when I was just 16 and the anniversary of her death was November 20th. Even worse, my due date for the baby we lost would have been November 17th. I knew it was going to be extremely tough to get through that time.

I had been keeping in contact with the birth mother of two of our children because they were distantly related to us through marriage. She was pregnant again and had planned to keep the baby. She gave birth in early October. I found out two weeks later that the baby had been taken into custody by Child Protective Services at the hospital and was in foster care in another part of the state. The mother called me and asked if we would take her if we could work it out through CPS. We didn't hesitate.

The state was very willing to place the baby, a girl, with us because we were in the process of adopting her older brother and sister. One week to the day before my due date for the baby we lost, CPS brought this baby girl to us. She was five weeks old. It seemed that God was determined I was going to have a baby to hold at that time! She has just turned five years old and both sides of our families are just astounded at how much like us she is.

Strangers constantly tell me how much she resembles me, having no idea she is adopted. Two years later we were blessed to add one more child to our family, the baby sister of our other sibling group. We have now have 6 beautiful children, ages 3 to 13. With a newborn, I knew there was no way I was going to go back to working outside the home. Two months later, I started a freelance writing business and that business has now grown to the point that I am able to work part-time from home and net more money than I earned in my management position.

My miscarriage dramatically changed my life. It took me a long time to come to peace with it. There was so much anger that I would lose my baby as well as the chance to ever get pregnant again. It really did take me a long time to work through all of that but I finally came to understand that we do not live in a perfect world. Until Christ returns we are not immune to bad things happening. The adversary is very much out there and loves nothing better than to hurt God's children.

Despite that, God blessed us more than I could ever imagine. I still think about the baby we lost and while I would have dearly loved to hold that baby in my arms, I really am at peace about it now.

Men's Stories

Women are not the only ones who struggle after having a miscarriage. Many men grieve too, although they usually do it in a way that is more difficult to detect.

Jason's Story

When I found out Sandi was having a miscarriage, I was devastated. He would have been our third child. We had never had any problems with any of our other pregnancies, why this one. I knew that my wife Sandi would be crushed and that I had to be strong for her. It might sound sappy, but I love babies. Every time my wife was pregnant I felt like a kid on Christmas Eve. I could not wait for the baby to be born. I was in disbelief. These things don't happen to us...do they? I didn't want to believe it.

When Sandi knew there were problems, she got her Mom to go with her to the doctor. I was at work and met her there. I got there a little late and Sandi already knew by the time I walked in the door. I could tell by the look on her face that he was gone. I bit back the tears while Sandi cried on my shoulder. She drove home and I had to go back to work. I went in to work and told them I had to go home. I explained what happened and left. This entire time I kept my composure. On the 30 minute drive home it happened. I felt more alone than ever. I cried for the next half hour. I could not believe our baby was gone. I thought about how I never got to tell him that I loved him. A million things went through my mind over and over again. I have always had a little poet in me and I started putting together a poem in my mind describing how I was feeling. When I got home I put it on paper. I found it very easy to grieve with my wife. I never considered myself very emotional, but this was over the top. I needed Sandi more than ever and at the same time, I had to be strong for her.

I feel that Sandi and I reacted similarly. I will say that she probably let her emotions out more than I did, but that was only because I had to fight back the urge to breakdown so that I could be there for her. She had enough to deal with without having to worry about me.

If I was going to give any advice to other fathers who have gone through this, I would say: Open up with your spouse. She is the only one who is going to understand exactly how you feel. Men always think they have to be strong, and to a point we fake that a lot. Your wife will admire how much the loss affects you. She will see that she is not alone with the pain. That will help you both to heal with time.

<u>In Loving Memory Of Our Baby</u>

Although you were only,

just 2 months in the womb,

I had wonderful thoughts of joy,

that you would be coming soon.

And though I know you were a gift

from my Lord above,

the only gift I could ever give you,

was that of your Daddy's love.

now that you are gone,

I will mourn for you.

Your mommy and sisters, they will mourn too.

Our memory of you will never go away.

We long to be heaven,

with you again someday.

Love,

Daddy

Ken's Story

My wife and I lost two children through miscarriage.

Unlike my wife, I never had any physical connection with the children and because of that 'lack' I had no emotional connection of which I was aware at the time.

My attention was focused on Mona's response to the loss. She experienced the full gamut of emotions associated with grief: guilt, anger, remorse, helplessness, loss, etc.

I did not experience those same emotions.

But even today when we sit down together for a meal and I count heads and all five surviving children are present I am still aware that some are missing.

The loss is real and it never goes away.

The other loss that is real is the son from a prior relationship that I lost to abortion. I was a willing accomplice in his death.

I never assumed responsibility for his conception and I contributed financially to his death.

After Mona and I were married I told her about my other life before Christ.

I have not yet been able to tell my five surviving children that they have a half brother whom they will never know in this life.

They are all old enough now where we can have that conversation. I believe it is overdue.

Steve's Story

My wife, Sara, and I have one son, Benjamin. He turned 3 earlier this month. We are actually pretty lucky to have him. Sara got her progesterone checked early on in his pregnancy and it was very low. She was put on medication and we went to the doctor regularly because of it. We had more ultrasounds than most people would ever get. We were both pretty nervous and paranoid throughout the whole pregnancy. We went to the hospital twice thinking she was having the baby prematurely, but fortunately it didn't happen.

The due date came up and nothing was going on. The baby was very big, so the doctor decided to give her medication to help it go faster. It ended up going so quickly that the doctor didn't even make it to the hospital to deliver the baby. A nurse actually did it (her first time going solo).

In the room were the two moms, me, and the nurse (and many some other technicians, but my memory is vague). They didn't even get the stirrups out. I helped up one leg and her mom held the other. The baby's head got stuck and it was a challenge to get Ben out. He was born perfectly normal and all was well.

3-4 months ago we decided to start trying again for baby number two. Sara went on pre-natal vitamins a few weeks in advance and did all the things she was supposed to. We are pretty sure the baby was conceived quickly. (We think so with Benjamin too). The OB doctor wanted to keep a close eye on Sara because of the issues last time. She went on progesterone. They checked her HCG levels and they were low, checked again and they did not double; in fact, they barely moved at all.

They continued to check levels about five times. After the fifth time, they told her it was not looking good and there was a good chance of a miscarriage and actually told her at that point what some of her options would be, and said that if she has any issues to go to the ER. Later that evening, we did go to the ER. I think it was mainly just because of nerves and our hope to find something out.

The ER doctor did an ultrasound and didn't see anything. The OB thought it might be a tubal pregnancy and could hurt my wife. So the ER doctor called in the sonogram technician. He was able to find something. It was not in the tubes - it was where it was suppose to be. The heart beat was a little low, other than that, the ER doctor thought we were in good shape. She (ER doctor) told us that she doesn't understand why OB doctors nowadays test HCG so much (I guess they never did it in the past). She said it is not worth the worry.

We went to the OB doctor a week later. The heartbeat was better, but there was a little blood around the sac and it was measuring a little smaller than it should, but still not too bad (about 7 weeks). We were told to come back in 10 days.

9 days later Sara started to bleed a little so we went in a day sooner than scheduled. The sonogram tech at the OB office did an ultrasound, but didn't really talk much, so we became nervous.

The doctor came in and pretty much right away said that there was no heartbeat and that the baby was measuring smaller than it should be. My wife and I held hands. Disappointment was clearly on our faces.

The doctor went over our options: give it five or more days and see what happens naturally, or do a D&C. The doctor left us for a moment to talk. We hugged and cried a little, but hold most of it in.

Sara wanted to be over and chose to have the surgery as soon as possible. We got it scheduled for the next morning.

I called my parents to let them know. This is when I pretty much lost it and started crying. I then went to work to get my computer and let my boss know I would be out for the week. I asked my co worker if she could cover for me and she asked if everything was OK. I shook my head and tried to tell her what was happening. Again, I lost it.

It took me about 20 seconds to say "*My wife was pregnant and we lost the baby.*" It is weird because I can keep composure well, but when I have to say it out loud, I just can't. The miscarriage actually wasn't a huge surprise to me. After the first call said there were problems with the HCG levels I had an attitude where I "expected the worst, but hoped for the best." After what we went through in the first pregnancy, I would think, "I can't expect this is going to work unless someone tells me, 'yes, everything is going great!'"

We know a few people that recently had miscarriages too. When they told me about them, I used to say "I am so sorry, I can't imagine what you are going through." Now I *do* know, and now I understand just how hard it was for them. Before we found out Sara was pregnant I would typically pray every other day or so. But after I found out she was pregnant, I prayed every morning in the shower, on the commute home from work, and before bed. I told God to watch over Sara and our baby, and that I would die for both of them if I had to... and I really meant that.

Sara and I haven't really talked much about it, which I know it probably not healthy. It is still early, so I need to work on that. I want to know how we will remember our baby. We don't know our baby's name nor sex. He/she was barely 9 weeks. I wish he/she had a name so I can pray and say a name rather than him/her. Like I said earlier, unless I say it out loud, I don't show a lot of emotion, but once I have to say, my wife had a miscarriage, I let it all out.

My wife is the same way. She is strong, but I think in the next day or two, we need to talk about it. At that point, I am sure the emotions will get out. After the surgery, when she was pretty high on medication, she told me "Sorry for letting you down." I told her it wasn't anyone's fault.

The hospital gave us some pretty neat stuff...some brochures, little charm, and a medallion of Jesus on a rocking chair with a baby in his hands. I assume we will keep that forever. I want to talk to her about how we will remember this baby (our second child). I say it is our second child even though we never really saw him/her.

My Miscarriage Story

(The following was copied straight from my online journal, from February 19, 2007 to July 6, 2007.)

February 19, 2007

I never thought this would happen to me :-(

Just to let you know, this will be an emotional post.

Today, I went to the doctor to get my ultrasound made... I had planned to tell my children about the baby after getting the pictures. I was getting so excited about it!

I drove to my moms and dropped the kids off, then went to the doctor, and waited my turn. Then I got the ultrasound done...

I noticed something strange while I was there...the nurse looked kind of worried and she kept looking around for a lot longer than I'm used to for this stage of pregnancy. (I'm only about 8-10 weeks). She then said, "*I can't seem to find a heartbeat.*"

I didn't think much about it at first, because that has happened before, and it was always a false alarm. So I figured that the ultrasound just wasn't able to pick it up, maybe the placenta was in the way, etc. Whatever the case was, I wasn't worried...I just *knew* my baby was safe and sound. I've never had a problem before.

The lady who did the ultrasound took about 25 pictures ...I was surprised to see so many coming out of the machine, and commented about it....she replied that at this point in pregnancy, they usually take a lot, so they can check the ovaries and stuff. I was satisfied with that, and thought nothing more of it.

Then she said that she'd like me to see the doctor that was on call that day, since my doctor was not in. I said ok, and waited in the waiting room with a magazine for a while.

Then, in came the new doctor.

She asked me how I was doing, shook my hand, and then told me that she was sorry to have to be the one to tell me this, but my baby's brain was not developing normally.

At this point, I thought, ok, so my baby might have a disability. That was not a problem for me. The thought of anything worse had not occurred to me.

<u>Then she continued, and said that my baby did not have a heartbeat, and had unfortunately *passed away*.....</u>

She made sure to make it clear that my baby was not alive anymore, and had already passed on in my womb. She apologized for having to tell me a second time for having to be the one to "break the news".

I stood there just looking at her, not really comprehending what she had said. I mean, this couldn't be happening. Not to me. I hadn't done anything to cause something like this....or had I? How could this be possible?

I asked her if she was absolutely sure, that there was no possible doubt in her mind...I thought maybe I could change her mind and I wanted to hear her say it was not really the case...

She said no, however, and then she went on to tell me that it was probably God's will, trying to make me feel better.

At that point though, I just didn't know what to think. I was numb and didn't know how to react. I just said, thanks, and walked out of the room.

I thought I had handled things well, until I kept looking at the ultrasound she handed to me. My mind was racing with all kinds of thoughts. My stomach started to feel like it was in knots.

I handed the papers to the secretary to get my next appointment card. It seemed like it took her forever to get it done. I kept thinking, please hurry, please hurry. I realized if she didn't hurry up, I was going to break down and cry right there. But the secretary didn't hurry.

Suddenly, my eyes began to well up with tears. The secretary asked me a question as I was turned away from her, and I immediately turned around to answer her question, and when she saw my eyes with tears falling from them, she looked concerned... I couldn't help or contain it anymore once that happened, and I just started weeping right there. I couldn't control myself...I tried so hard to hold it in.

There was a lady behind me who saw me crying and immediately put her arm around me and tried to console me...she asked me what was the matter. Trying to tell her what it was was so difficult. I could barely get the words out. I finally managed to choke out, "They told me...my baby...is......dead."   And then I went into another fit of tears. My body was trembling so hard, and I could hear the two ladies feeling sorry for me, and I didn't want them to feel bad. But I couldn't stop crying.

The ladies asked me if there was anyone they could call, or if I would like to talk to anyone. They asked me if I'd like to sit down. I kept trying to tell them I was okay, but I kept choking it out and it sounded so weepy it was too unbelievable to them.

They told me to please call someone to take me home, because they didn't think I needed to drive myself home feeling like that. So I asked them to call James for me.   He asked what the matter was, and I couldn't even tell him. My hands were shaking so hard and I managed to bring the words out that I would tell him what the matter was when he got there. It was just too hard to say the words!

It seemed like it took forever for him to get there.   I paced around, and hid in the snack room in the hospital, and would start crying, then I'd stop, and then I'd start again, and I'd look at the ultrasound picture, and start crying again.

I finally saw him through the window and he came in and I just hugged him really tight and started gasping and crying. He held me and I think he probably knew what was coming, but I finally was able to tell him. We got into the car and shared a few moments hugging and crying together.

James ended up taking off work so that he could be with me today...which I really appreciated. It meant a lot for me that he was there for me. I know that it hurt him a lot too, knowing what had happened.

So that is how today has gone. It seems like the last couple of months have had some hardships and this is probably the hardest thing I've had to face in a long time. I don't know when I'll be delivering the baby. It'll probably be sometime in the next 4 weeks. I'll be going to the doctor again tomorrow for a blood test to see when it'll happen.   I'm going to let it happen naturally...no D & C for me...I don't like the idea at all.

It's really sad, but I have to remember that God gives and He takes away, according to His wisdom. There's a purpose for everything, and I know that there is a purpose in this, no matter how hard it may be to see at this time. Just pray for us, that we'll be able to heal emotionally...and please pray that when the baby does miscarry, that it won't be too painful.

FEBRUARY 20, 2007

Thank you so much

Thank you all so much for your kind words, emails, calls, and prayers. I feel so blessed to have people all over, some who don't even really know me, who are all so concerned and really care about what I'm going through. Thank you, most of all, for taking the time to pray.

Last night, I tried to sleep but was awake all night trying to put the pieces together. Before I had gone to bed, I was able to push it out of my mind by watching funny TV shows and talking to James about funny things that the kids do, but the second I laid on the pillow, tears started falling again.

I just kept trying to comprehend it all. I kept trying to go to sleep, but looked at the clock as it changed from hour to hour to hour. Finally, I got up out of bed at 6:00 and made some orange juice. I did notice my morning sickness was not there like usual. I had noticed the last couple of weeks it has been dying down and getting much better, but before yesterday, I just thought that I was "lucky" this time. I thought it was just ending a little earlier or something. I haven't felt the urge to throw up in a while (though I do still get nauseous slightly).

James seemed worried to leave me this morning; I could see in his eyes that he wanted to stay. He gave me a long hug and told me to have a good day. He's such a good husband, and has made things so much easier on me...without him I don't know what I'd do.

There's no one else I really feel comfortable letting all my emotions out with. With most people, I will try to avoid crying or revealing my true emotions at all costs... but with him, I can tell him anything and it doesn't matter. If someone calls me and asks me how I'm doing, I just tell them I'm ok, that I'll be fine...it's too hard to tell them how I feel because I know I'll start crying and I don't want them to hear me crying. I guess I just don't want to burden them. I'll just avoid bringing any emotion into the conversation at all. But with James, he knows everything in my heart.

Today I'll be getting a blood test done to check my levels... I guess that this blood test combined with another one in the future will be what truly confirms what they've said. I would love to think they made some kind of mistake, but I would be foolish to get my hopes up and then get them crushed again.

My sister is very sweet...last night she told me that she's baking me some oatmeal butterscotch cookies and bringing them over.

I guess today I'll be researching some on how to handle a natural miscarriage, and what to expect. I know for sure that a D & C is not an option for me. The idea that the same people who do those also perform abortions...it's too hard for me to handle. Plus, there are so many risks with a D & C, and I'm not convinced it's a less painful alternative... and it can cause infertility which would be a horrible thing to go through. I know that a lot of people do it and have no problems, but I just can't take that chance.

James just called as I was typing, and he was checking on me to see how I'm doing. He's such a sweet heart.

Thanks again for all your thoughts and prayers and I hope you all have a wonderful day.

FEBRUARY 21, 2007

My appointment yesterday

Yesterday, my appointment was at 3:00. I thought that I was going to have a blood test done, but when I got there, I realized they only wanted to talk to me and get my questions and figure out what I wanted to do next. I guess that they have no doubt as to their conclusion.

My doctor, who I've only seen once before, came in, and was so much more sympathetic than the other doctor who was on call the day before. I remember that doctor was so textbook like and cold that I had a hard time understanding what she was relaying to me.

My doctor was so much more kind and understanding. She walked in and the first thing she did was to give me a hug and give her sympathies. She also told me that she had suffered from two miscarriages, and she gave me a booklet that she said had helped her heal through them.

She went through everything and explained all my options. She was much less "pro - D & C" than the other doctor, though she herself had had a D & C for both of her miscarriages. The other doctor had made me feel that a miscarriage at home would be much more risky and painful, but my doctor told me that the risks are the exact same for both. She did say that most people who have a natural miscarriage do end up going to the ER at 1:00 in the morning.... but I asked her if that was because they were really in danger, or because they were in pain and scared...she said it was the latter. She said that it is not usually any more risky to do it at home. It's just very painful. That gave me a LOT of comfort in my decision to stay at home and do this naturally.

I asked her if she could prescribe me some pain medication so that I could cope with the pain if it got too painful, and she did prescribe me some pain pills.

She told me if I changed my mind, that she could set the D & C as early as today. But I just can't go that route. I just can't. I would always be wondering if the baby had been alive and I had actually aborted it.
If I am going to have a miscarriage, I'm going to let it happen on it's own.

I started thinking about this on the way home, and I asked James what he thought we should do with the body when it comes out...I was really worried about what to do with it - I wouldn't want to just throw it away...it's my baby.

He told me that we can bury our baby in the yard, and plant a tree, that way it wouldn't feel like the baby has just been forgotten. When he said that, it just made me cry because it was such a sweet thought but also really sad to think about. I definitely want to do that... that way every time I see that tree I will remember my baby.

I am still having pregnancy symptoms, but from what I've read on miscarriage websites, that is supposed to be normal, because your body still doesn't recognize the death of the baby yet.... until that happens, I could still be having them for a while. It's kind of hard because I do want to think that I'm still pregnant with a live baby, but I just don't think it would be wise to keep that kind of hope alive.

So for the next couple of days, weeks, maybe a month or more, I'll be waiting for this to happen. I have no idea when it will be, but hopefully when it comes I'll be prepared for it.

FEBRUARY 23, 2007

Voice recital yesterday, ended in tears

Yesterday, I had been feeling fine the whole day, laughing and cutting up with people and things like that. My mom took me out to a great new Deli that just opened up, and the food was delicious.

I had to go to my voice recital at 3:00, so after eating lunch, she took the kids with her to her house, and I left for college.

I got there, and listened to all the other students singing their songs. Most of the music that is sung in these lessons is classical or religious music... so halfway through the recital, I started to feel uneasy and a little bit emotional. I just wanted to go home and lay down. I went from being happy to being sad in an instant.

The teacher called me up to sing my song, which just happens to be a song from Psalms...a cry to God during emotional times. Halfway through the song, when I heard myself singing, "When my heart is overwhelmed, lead me to the Rock that is higher than I", my voice went out. I know the students just thought that I couldn't hit that note, but I was about to cry. I had to force myself not to, reminding myself that if I cried, I might have to explain to all those people there why I was crying.

I sang the rest of the song, doing a better job through the next part, but as soon as I got down to my seat, tears started welling in my eyes. I had to keep wiping them away, and trying to hide it from everyone else. I was in the back but there were a few people who might have seen. When the recital was over, I went to the bathroom to cry a little bit more and then I powdered my face and reapplied my makeup, and walked toward the door to leave....

when I passed the office where my teacher was by then, she said, "Hi Bethany!" I walked back by the office to reply, and said "Hi."   Then I apologized to her for messing up during the song. I felt bad about it, because I have never had a problem with that song.   She told me that sometimes that just happens and that it was ok... And I said, "yeah I've just had a hard week"...or, that's what I TRIED to say.   What I ended up doing was crying that whole sentence.

And then I was so embarrassed that I had started crying again that I started to walk towards the door and then she realized I was really sad and she said, "Oh my gosh. Bethany, are you ok?"
She closed the door and sat down and gave me a Kleenex and asked what the matter was.

I really didn't want to burden her. I am so not used to crying in front of people... I try to avoid it at all costs... but as soon as she started giving me compassion, I couldn't turn it off. It just kept coming. I kept telling myself, *"control yourself, control yourself. Just stop crying, she doesn't need to be burdened with my problems, just calm down"*, but I couldn't do what I wanted to do.

I ended up telling her the whole story...and it was hard to choke out. She was very understanding and she told me that some things to try to comfort me...one of them was that sometimes God knows things that *we don't know*. And sometimes there are things we just don't understand but God does understand.

I do understand that and believe it with all my heart. I guess it just doesn't help me to not be sad though. I must still have to grieve a while, regardless of the logical knowledge that God knows best.

Anyway, I had thought that I was "over it"....not really over it, but at least over the extreme sad feelings...I thought I could at least control myself around people, but I guess not yet.

I wonder how long I will feel this pain. I never would have thought that I could have been this emotional about a baby that I haven't even seen, at this early of a stage. I have always believed that it would make me sad if it ever happened, but I never realized the extent to which it hurts you, deep down.

I wonder if people think I'm crazy for being this sad over a miscarriage.... I don't know. It's hard to understand until you go through it. I know that I was only 8 weeks, but I believe with all my heart that baby is just as important as if he or she were full term and passed away.

I'm also worried about what is to come, and how long it will be before I deliver the baby. The doctor told me it could be anytime....so far though, I am still having pregnancy symptoms, and still having NO cramping and NO bleeding. I keep hoping it will just happen so that I can move on and heal from this. I hope that it will happen this week. I wanted to have the baby tested to see if it was a boy or a girl but then realized that if I did that, I would not get my baby back. I would not be able to bear that...the baby must be buried close by.

I will never know whether it would have been a girl or a boy, but I do know that it was my baby, my precious baby who lives in Heaven now...one day I will get to meet my baby and understand why this had to happen.

FEBRUARY 24, 2007

Yesterday

Yesterday, I kept busy all day... I scrubbed out the bathtub and bleached it, cleaned the kitchen out, scrubbed the floors, bleached the counters, went outside and picked up two bags of garbage the stray dogs had strewn all over the yard. Ugh those dogs are annoying.

I did a few loads of laundry, cleaned up the living room, and I played with the kids on the swing set... they had so much fun and were all laughing and we had such a good time out there...it was warm enough to go barefoot and no sleeves. When I came in, I made chocolate peanut butter squares. Then I made some potato salad and some chicken and dumplings for supper.

I realized that if I keep busy, it really helps! So I'm just going to keep busy until the day comes that I have to deal with the miscarriage. I was so tired by 8:30 that James and I just went to bed then. I felt so much more cheerful than I had felt the whole week. It was nice. I had felt badly about neglecting the kids the last week....having to be gone to the doctor so much and then coming home and being depressed...they weren't getting much "mommy time", so I decided to change that.

Yesterday afternoon, I noticed some spotting. I don't know if it is significant or not though, because I had a catheter Thursday, when I got my second ultrasound and opinion. That may have caused that to happen, but I'm not sure. It hasn't happened again, so I'll just wait and see.

Today I am planning to get a lot of cleaning done...lots of clothes folded and put away. I want to get a drawing finished that I have put on the back burner.... and finish painting something I had intended to be James' birthday present, but didn't finish it in time.   Maybe I'll get a chance to watch a movie with the kids too.

By the way, I haven't responded to all the comments, but I have read each and every one. Every comment has made such a difference and has impacted me in such a positive way. I appreciate all of your kind words so much more than you'll ever know!   Thank you so much for caring and praying....I don't know how to tell you how much it means to me that you care!

February 25, 2007

James took me out last night

Last night, James took me to Ruby Tuesday, as his brother watched all three of the kids for us. We ate a great meal...the steak there is absolutely delicious...so tender. I like it a little bit on the rare side, and mine turned out perfect. James ordered the Tilapia with shrimp. It looked really good too.

It was nice to get a little bit of time alone, so that could relax and not worry about watching the kids for a while, and was able to talk with James...it was just really nice. We went to the store and were looking around at the trees they have there. We found the perfect tree to memorialize our little one...it will be a willow...either a *Japanese Weeping Willow*, or a *Snow Fountain Willow*. Both are equally beautiful and I think this kind of tree represent the feelings that we both have about losing this baby.

It brought me so much comfort somehow knowing that we will have such a beautiful tree planted in memorial of the baby. To know that my husband puts just as much value on the baby as I do really means a lot to me. I am so thankful that God gave such a man to me.

I had Italian Herb bread rising when I got back home, and I baked it and it turned out so soft and beautiful. I just love that bread! My family can't get enough of it either...as soon as it came out of the oven, everyone was begging for pieces of it.

March 1, 2007

I think it could happen soon

I think the miscarriage could happen soon. I've been having some indicators that it could be on the way...but I do not know how long the wait will be. I feel that it will be within the next 7 days, if not today or tomorrow.

Last night I realized that things were coming into place for it to happen, and I once again began to feel emotional about it, and I cried and cried into my pillow.

I am mostly scared because I do not know exactly what to expect....I am at a point where I just really want it to come, but at the same time, I don't want it to happen at all! However, I know that it's not in my control.

I have a feeling of helplessness because I know it is inevitable now. Even though I knew it was certain to come before, it seemed like it became more clear to me last night.

MARCH 2, 2007

I have finally found closure

Last night, at about 1:50, the baby finally miscarried. I was going to post the whole story of how it happened and everything, but was afraid that some of it would be too graphic for some, and didn't want to offend anyone. If you happen to want to know the story, I will be happy to share it with you though. Just send me an email.

My miscarriage was actually almost pain free, thank the Lord!
   I did have some monthly type cramping, but that is all. I know that pain will continue until everything has passed, but it's nothing I can't handle.
I do have to let you know that my baby was so amazing, and I was in awe at God's creation!! All the fingers and toes were there, and they were perfect! ....the baby was the size of a little bean.... looked so much like those pictures you can find on the internet[13]...

I think that the baby must have been 6 weeks when he or she

---

[13] (Note: I received several emails from women who felt tremendous guilt for not having been able to find their babies during their miscarriages. I just want to tell you that if you were not able to find your baby during your miscarriage, *please do not blame yourself.* You did nothing wrong.

It is not very common to be able to find the baby during a miscarriage; very few women actually do. Please remember that no matter whether you find the baby or not, your baby was still real.)

died.   God gave me the grace last night to handle it all, and I truly feel that I have been given a peace somehow through, after having gone through this.

I don't know why, but for some reason, actually seeing the baby is what brought me closure. I felt an overwhelming sense of relief once I saw it.... I can't figure out why that would be, but I am thankful.

My husband was asleep as I went through the rest of the miscarriage, and when he awoke in the morning, I told him what had happened. He said he was thankful for my sake that it had happened quickly and without too much pain.   He could not look at the baby though. I think that for him, it would be too hard to see that. I did take pictures which I will not show him unless he asks. I did not want to forget what the baby looked like.

I have the baby in a little jewelry box that I bought especially for this day, and we'll be planting the tree (we decided on the Snow Fountain Willow) tonight.

 This journal has been so therapeutic for me in dealing with my loss, and I appreciate you all staying there as I talked about my feelings and cried.

I think that from this day on, I should be feeling much, much better. I know that your prayers have had such an impact on me and my family!

Thanks again for all the kind words and thoughts.

MARCH 3, 2007

My husband once again surprises me

My hubby continually surprises me with how thoughtful and caring he can be.

Last night, he went to the store to buy the flowering willow tree for our memorial. He called me and said that Lowe's didn't have what we needed, and he had to go to another town to get the one that we were looking for.

When James got back from the store, he and his brother went outside for a little bit, and I figured they were talking about where the best place would be to put the tree. I was making dinner, so I couldn't go out there at that time.

I finally did come out with a flashlight, after they had been out there a while. I noticed that they were carrying not one, but *two* trees with them over on our field.

I was confused but kept watching.... they put the trees down, turned around, went back to the truck, and got TWO MORE trees out of the truck!

I said to my husband, "Wow! You got *four trees*?"

He said, "Actually, there's one more in the truck!", and he gave me a happy smile. Then he told me what his plan was.... he had bought one of the Japanese weeping cherry willow trees for the center, where the baby would be buried. But he bought four of the Snow fountain cherry willows to place around the weeping cherry tree....at four corners around the tree!

James told me that when he got there and was going to purchase the tree, he felt that one tree just wouldn't be enough.   It just wasn't enough for something so special.

He and his brother spent about 2 hours with the trees to get them perfectly aligned and spaced out. Then they planted the four on the corners themselves while I fed the kids supper and cleaned up.

When they were finished planting the four trees on the corners, they left the last one for James and me to go out and plant alone....and James brother watched our kids for us (they were already sleeping by the time we went out there).

We went out with our flashlight and a lantern, and the box which carried our baby, "Blessing".

James had already dug out the hole, and we placed the box then the tree inside and covered them...then we sat for a few moments holding each other and talking about how we felt. We then took a walk around our block just talking. It was so nice to have that alone time with him.

They may not look like much right now, but the trees are going to be absolutely gorgeous when they bloom next year.   Also, this morning, James' mother gave us a beautiful, bright red tulip to plant beside the center tree.   It really, really stands out, and it should spread out over the years.

MARCH 6, 2007

My baby's life was not in vain

Today, I went to the local pregnancy crisis center, and I asked them if they could possibly use the pictures of my baby.. I wondered if there was any way it could help the pro-life cause.
   There are about a dozen of the pictures, and I put all of the best ones on a CD...one of them with a Bible verse on it (Psalm 139:13-16).

The woman at the pregnancy center almost cried when she saw the pictures...she gave me a hug, and said they could definitely use them...in fact, she wanted to know if it might be ok for her to use the pictures when she goes to speak at a College soon. She gave me a little pin to wear on my shirt...it is a tiny gold replica of baby feet. They are made to be the exact size of the baby feet of a 10 week old unborn child. They are beautiful.

She told that she was sorry for my loss, she knew it had to be hard....and she wondered what made me decide to come out and bring the pictures. I told her that it's been very hard dealing with the miscarriage, but I felt that if something good can come out of it, I could feel like my baby had not died in vain.

If my baby's loss could be used to prevent other babies from dying, it would make it all worth the pain I've gone through. I think most people are not aware of how *real* unborn babies are, even from the beginning, and sometimes textbook pictures aren't enough to help people really understand the reality of life in the womb. I think that by women who are considering abortion, seeing pictures that are actually real and personal....I think that might have more impact than other pictures might have. At least I hope that it would.

MARCH 11, 2007

The trees are blooming!

I noticed yesterday that the trees we planted, in memorial of our little one, are already starting to bloom!! Two of the Snow Fountain Cherry Willows are already blooming and are beautiful!

I can't wait to see them all in bloom.

MARCH 15, 2007

The middle tree is blooming now

I was so happy yesterday to see the tree (where the baby is buried) finally blooming. It is so beautiful.
The other trees are all starting to bloom also. But the middle tree is the prettiest.

Last week, I ordered another pendant to go on my birthstone baby necklace[14] that James bought me last year.

---

[14] I got the pendant at http://www.PersonalizationMall.com.

JUNE 19, 2007

I have the most incredible news!

Today, I went to the doctor about the dizzy spells and fatigue I have been having for the past few days. The symptoms have been going on for a few weeks.

When I got there, I showed him the results of the tests, and he said that except for the 35, the rest appears to be normal. I personally think that the 35 was a mistaken test... So that is a relief that I am most likely not having any blood sugar problems.

When I got to the pregnancy center today (I don't know if I have mentioned here that I have begun working at a Crisis Pregnancy Center several weeks ago?), I was sitting there and wondering what the problem could be. No one had come in for a couple of hours, so I had plenty of time to sit and think.

I considered the idea that it could actually be the inner ear problem, since I have been having sinus allergy problems lately.

And then I remembered that I had spotted the day before yesterday, strangely. My menstrual cycle ended only 2 weeks ago. But for some reason, I had this weird idea to take a pregnancy test. I thought to myself, "why would I waste a pregnancy test? I am definitely not pregnant.", but for some reason I felt compelled to do it anyway.

I went into the bathroom and I took the test. I left it in the room and went into the other room to read a book for a little bit, then I went back in to check on the test.

When I came in the room and saw the test, I gasped in unbelief. There were two VERY bold lines on the test.

I just stood there in shock looking at it and thinking, "no way, this cant' be happening". I just didn't think it was possible.

Then I ran to the phone and called James. I told him excitedly and then as soon as I got off the phone I started blubbering and crying. I paced back and forth and I don't know why but I just couldn't stop crying. It was a mixture of pure joy and thankfulness, but also sadness for the baby I lost and will never get to see grow up.

I am so excited, thrilled, and thankful! I am so thankful that I have been blessed with another pregnancy, but I am going to be so cautious with this one. I can't just take it for granted that this baby will make it....Please pray that my baby will be safe and sound through this pregnancy.

June 20, 2007

Just not sure

Today I went to the doctor, and she seemed just as mystified as I was about the fact that I had a period just two weeks ago and the HCG levels are high enough to test positive on a test. Especially since it happened right on time and seemed completely normal. She took my blood and will be taking it again Friday to compare the levels and see if they are rising or dropping. I'm concerned. I have been searching online for answers.   I found many places saying that if you spot after 2 weeks you probably miscarried early, too early for most people to detect it. I don't know if that's true or not because the line was so bold. I also saw other sites that said some women have what seems to be a period and actually isn't, right at the beginning of their pregnancy...and their pregnancy turns out fine.   I guess what I will have to do is wait and see what the doctor thinks...I wont know till Monday how the blood tests compare.

June 21, 2007

Blood HCG levels

Okay, I finally got a call from the doctor. She told me that the levels that she was going to give me are not by themselves a perfect indicator of how far along I am at this time, because I have to compare it with tomorrow's blood HCG levels, but she said that the number of the level is 1529. She said this would typically mean that I am probably 2-3 weeks long...so that's how far along I could be, but we won't know until she does it again. I also won't know if this baby is thriving or not till I get the results back Monday. But at least I know *something*.

I wish I could get rid of the butterflies in my stomach feeling though....

June 22, 2007

Comfort

This blog makes a great place to post my feelings. Once I post about something, especially if it's been bothering me, I usually feel a lot better about it. It's a way for me to get that worry "out of me".

Today I feel much more at peace about the whole situation. I believe that things will happen the way they should.
The butterfly feeling I mentioned isn't so much fear and stress as it is confusion. I find it difficult to know how I should be reacting at this time. For instance, should I be grieving another loss? Or should I be rejoicing about my pregnancy? I really want to be rejoicing, and I think that this butterfly in my stomach feeling is me holding back the excitement of being pregnant again. I just want to let it out.

The day I saw the two lines, I was yelling to James "I can't believe it, I saw two lines!" and was so excited. When he got home he told me I am getting excited too quickly. He doesn't want to see me go through the pain he saw me go through last time- he's trying to protect me. I can tell he wants to be excited about it also, but is too afraid that expressing that would hurt me in the long run.

I understand where he's coming from... I was so excited. He is probably right, I should not get too attached to the idea of having another baby until I can be more sure that I'm actually going to stay pregnant. And that is most likely why I feel so anxious. I just want to know for sure. Knowing one way or the other is easier than not knowing anything.

But I do have a good feeling about this, and a sense of peace. I think it could be due to the prayers of all my friends out there.

Isaiah 38:17

"Behold, it was for my welfare that I had great bitterness; but in love you have delivered my life from the pit of destruction, for you have cast all my sins behind your back."

Philippians 4:4-8

"Rejoice in the Lord always; again I will say, Rejoice. Let your reasonableness be known to everyone. The Lord is at hand; do not be anxious about anything, but in everything by prayer and supplication with thanksgiving let your requests be made known to God. And the peace of God, which surpasses all understanding, will guard your hearts and your minds in Christ Jesus.

Finally, brothers, whatever is true, whatever is honorable, whatever is just, whatever is pure, whatever is lovely, whatever is commendable, if there is any excellence, if there is anything worthy of praise, think about these things."

JUNE 25, 2007

The results I got today

This morning, I had one little spot of blood when I went to the bathroom.

My heart fell.

I went to the living room and cried and cried.

Then, after this, I decided that instead of calling for the results, I would go to the doctor in person. I went to the doctor and the receptionist told me that I couldn't see the results till tomorrow. I insisted that they had told me I would be able to see them Monday. I also told her about the spotting, and that I need to know what is going on.

She decided to see if she could get another doctor to do it. I sat in the waiting room and waited...finally I was in the doctor's office. The doctor told me that the levels had risen from Wednesday to Friday from 1529 to 2088. He said it should be doubling but it is not a cause for concern yet, because many women have carried pregnancies even with the levels rising slowly like this.

The doctor said that since the levels were 2088, they should be able to detect something with the ultrasound.

When I came in the room to get the ultrasound, the nurse there who was giving me the ultrasound said that I should not be alarmed if she didn't see anything on the monitor, since 2000 is a very early number...she said she wouldn't be surprised if she didn't see anything. And she didn't. She saw nothing whatsoever on the screen.

She reassured me, saying, "Don't worry, that doesn't mean you're not pregnant, it just means we did it early, and it's too small to be seen yet."

I went back to see the doctor, and he asked me when my last menstrual cycle was. I told him it was June 4th. He said that was more recent than he had thought. And he gave me two contrasting possibilities about what could be happening: He said that it is possible that I am carrying twins (my heart jumped at the thought), since my levels are so extremely high for how close my menstrual cycle was...and he also said it is possible that I miscarried since the last levels were taken. But I do not know how that would be possible, since I have only had one drop of blood since then. But I could be wrong....I don't know. I just don't know.

I don't think the doctor understood how much this has affected me emotionally. He seemed so distant and matter of fact about everything he said. He told me that we would have another blood test Friday, to see if the levels have gone up from last Friday, and then if they have gone up, we'll do another ultrasound.

I asked him if since I wouldn't be able to get the results till Monday if we did that, if it would be possible for me to get my blood taken Thursday instead of Friday, and he said,

"No, I think it would be better to wait the whole week."

I know he probably has good reason to do that...it's just so hard waiting that long.

My heart was so excited at the possibility of carrying twins...but simultaneously devastated at the thought that I may have miscarried again. I just hope that this week will pass quickly. I have no idea how I should feel!

June 29, 2007

I am crying!

Oh my goodness. I am just in shock and in tears. I don't know what to say, or think, or what....

THANK you for praying! Thank you so much!

I am still not sure but....I went in to get my blood levels checked. I have been having what I believe is exactly like a period, so I was sure that I had totally miscarried...I had no hope that the levels were going to do anything except go down.

I asked the lady who took my blood if she could possibly please let me know how I could get the results today, because I did not want to wait a whole weekend to know what the results are. She told me that if I would call at about 11:35, they should have the results in.

I called at about that time, and the receptionist there told me that they didn't have them in. I told her that I thought they would be in by then, and she said, no, I would have to wait for them to call me. Well, I thought about it, and 10 minutes later, I called again. I was desperate to know.

I waited on hold for about 10 minutes as the new receptionist looked for the doctors and asked them about the results. She said that they were in rooms at the time, but would be out shortly. She asked if they could just call me back with the results. I said, well, can they call me in about a half hour? I will be going into town soon."

She said, "Well, just give me a minute." and I waited another 10 minutes. All of a sudden, I heard the voice of my doctor on the phone (the one who has always been considerate and compassionate in this situation), and she said,

"Bethany, your levels are going up. _It looks like you're still pregnant!_"

I took in a sharp breath and didn't know what to say. Then I said, "How??? How can I be pregnant? I am bleeding and bleeding...it's just like my period! How can they be rising????"

She said, "Well sometimes you do bleed in pregnancy...", and she said, "Your levels were 1529 the first time, then they were over 2000, and now they are showing at 4000! This is wonderful!"

I started crying and crying and I said, "Oh my goodness, I can't believe it!!"

She said, "Do they have you scheduled for an ultrasound? If not, I'll get you scheduled for one next week."

I got an ultrasound scheduled and I have been crying and crying with joy..... I cannot believe this. It is almost too unreal!!!!!

July 1, 2007

Can't wait till tomorrow!

Tomorrow is finally the day of the ultrasound!! I feel like I have been waiting an eternity! The appointment will be in the afternoon. I'm just trying to keep busy so that tomorrow will come quickly!

July 4, 2007

Answer to a Question

I received a question this morning, and I'm going to try to answer it to the best of my ability:

Hi Bethany,

Your honestly and openness has amazed and touched me. And thank you for the photos of you baby, Blessing. Amazing and beautiful.

My husband and I were surprised and thrilled to fall pregnant naturally as we needed ovulation stimulation with our first, Benjamin, who is now 22 months.

But it doesn't look like it is 'meant to be'. I am going through the motions of having a miscarriage. Yesterday, I was told that this pregnancy is unlikely to continue. My levels were too low (only 64 at about 4 weeks) and had not increased enough after almost another week (to only 106 on Monday). I've got cramps and bleeding and the doctors are not hopeful.

I've been reading an Australian ministry website, and it is teaching very strongly about faith in God being instrumental in helping to prevent miscarriage. I'm at the point of starting to accept that it isn't going to work out this time, but this website seems to say that if I just want it enough and demand it of God, then I may be able to stop the miscarriage. What are your thoughts? What do you think is the purpose of these babies that don't make it?

Sorry for the hugeness of the life questions and given the state of things at your house at the moment, I completely understand if you don't manage to reply. I hope everything proceeds smoothly and peacefully for you and your family. Regards, Louise.

****

Louise, thank you for your kind words, and I am so sorry that you are going through a possible miscarriage. I do not know enough about levels to know whether your miscarriage is inevitable or not, but I do hope and pray that whatever happens, you will have a peace throughout your soul. I know this is a difficult time for you.

I took a look at the site you gave me. While I feel that many of the things said do hold much truth, something about the site bothers me. I feel that they place blame on mothers for their miscarriages. I do not feel that this is right.

I am not a Biblical scholar, but I have read the Bible much over the years. This site mentions many of the promises given by God to the Israelites when they were given the Promised Land. I believe that the "promised land" for them in that time was literal. God gave the Israelites these promises.

However, for us, I do not believe these promises apply in the *literal* sense, as in, a *literal* land of milk and honey on the earth. The "promised land", in my opinion (for us) is an analogy for Heaven. When we are in Heaven, no one will die, or be sick, and all tears will be wiped away. This is our promise from God. We have a promise of eternal life through Jesus Christ.

I feel that most of the Old Testament stories, while literally true, are analogies which help us to understand God's covenant for us today. For instance, Moses held up the bronze serpent on a stick (*Numbers 21:4-9*), so that the people could look on it to escape punishment and to be healed of their sickness. Today, we look to Christ to escape punishment and to live eternal life.

"And as Moses lifted up the serpent in the wilderness, so must the Son of Man be lifted up, that whoever believes in him may have eternal life."

I don't think that we should take promises that God gave others, and apply them literally to ourselves. We must look at who God is speaking to and understand how it applies to us today. Of course, like I said, I am no Biblical scholar and I could be wrong.

When Job went through all of his suffering, did he lose his family, his possessions, everything he ever held dear to himself, through any sin of his own?

God told Satan:
"Have you considered my servant Job, that there is none like him on the earth, a blameless and upright man, who fears God and turns away from evil?"

Satan replied (I'm paraphrasing), "Well the only reason he fears you is because you have built a hedge around him and made him safe. You have increased his goods and he is comfortable with you. If all of this was taken away, he would curse you."

God told Satan that he had the power to do whatever he would to Job, except take his life.

When Satan took all of Job's family, all of Job's livestock, Job's home, Job's land, Job's possessions, what did Job do? He said, "The Lord gave, and the Lord has taken away; blessed be the name of the Lord."

This story, I believe, was given to us to show us an example of how we can go through suffering, even losing the lives of the people we love dearly, for a purpose. This is not always the result of sin.

God rewarded Job after his suffering had ended, and I know that Job also was able to meet his family again in Heaven after he died (and I am absolutely certain that when he went to Heaven, he understood what the purpose was for losing them- God wipes all tears from our eyes). Our life is temporary here. We live here temporarily, and if we are saved, we go to Heaven. That is our hope. Our children when they die, they are in Heaven. We will meet them again, and I believe firmly that when we see them in Heaven, we will understand the reasons that they had to die. Their death is not their end!

When the disciples asked Jesus (*John 9:2*),

"Rabbi, who sinned, this man or his parents, that he was born blind?", what did Jesus tell them?

Jesus told them (*John 9:3*),

"It was not that this man sinned, or his parents, but that the works of God might be displayed in him."

I believe that the trials and the sufferings that we endure in this life are here for a purpose...we do not always understand what the purpose is. But I assure you that if you are a believer, all the suffering that you endure will be for God's glory, and will work together for your eventual good, and most likely, the good of others. "And we know that all things work together for good to them that love God, to them who are the called according to his purpose."

For what purpose was Joseph thrown into a well by his own brothers? And then sold into slavery?
At the time, I am sure he could have doubted God's love for him, and could have wondered why God would have allowed him to endure such suffering. After all, what kind of purpose could God have for him to be sold into slavery? We do not always understand God's reasoning.

I'm sure you remember what ended up happening. Joseph ended up being second in command to the Pharaoh, and he ended up preventing thousands and thousands of people from starving when the famine came.

There are so many examples of people suffering, and losing their loved ones in the Bible...and many times, it was not a direct result of their own sins. Yes, death is a result of sin...the sin that we are all born with.
But I am talking about the direct result of a particular sin that you committed, or a sin that your husband committed, etc. I do not believe that this is the reason that you might be miscarrying. Do you see what I am saying?

I would hate for any woman to blame herself for the death of her child. If a woman loses her born children, due to cancer, or a car wreck, or any other cause, we do not try to find and place blame on her for this...why are people trying to find blame in a woman for a miscarriage?   What a woman needs when she is miscarrying is comfort and peace and love, not blame. Blaming a woman for her miscarriage brings about unnecessary confusion, sorrow, worry, and fear.

Does God ever promise us that we will not have troubles on this earth?

No, there are multitudes of verses in the old and New Testament which deal with God's comfort through our **trials**. If our life was meant to be without trials, then there would be no need for these verses.

2 Corinthians 1:3-4

"Blessed be the God and Father of our Lord Jesus Christ, the Father of mercies and God of all comfort, who comforts us in all our affliction, so that we may be able to comfort those who are in any affliction, with the comfort with which we ourselves are comforted by God."

(It occurs to me through the above verse that perhaps one reason for my miscarriage was to give me the wisdom and understanding to acknowledge other women's pain through miscarriage, so that I will have the ability to comfort them, where without having the experience, I would have not had the ability).

2 Corinthians 12:9a

"But he said to me, 'My grace is sufficient for you, for my power is made perfect in weakness.'"

2 Corinthians 4:16-18

"So we do not lose heart. Though our outer self is wasting away, our inner self is being renewed day by day. For this light momentary affliction is preparing for us an eternal weight of glory beyond all comparison, as we look not to the things that are seen but to the things that are unseen. For the things that are seen are transient, but the things that are unseen are eternal. "

1 Peter 5:10

"And after you have suffered a little while, the God of all grace, who has called you to his eternal glory in Christ, will himself restore, confirm, strengthen, and establish you."

Romans 8:18

"For I consider that the sufferings of this present time are not worth comparing with the glory that is to be revealed to us."

Revelation 21:4

"He will wipe away every tear from their eyes, and death shall be no more, neither shall there be mourning, nor crying, nor pain anymore, for the former things have passed away."

James 1:2-4

"Count it all joy, my brothers, when you meet trials of various kinds, for you know that the testing of your faith produces steadfastness. And let steadfastness have its full effect, that you may be perfect and complete, lacking in nothing. If any of you lacks wisdom, let him ask God, who gives generously to all without reproach, and it will be given him."

Ecclesiastes 3:1-8

"For everything there is a season, and a time for every matter under heaven:
a time to be born, and a time to die;
a time to plant, and a time to pluck up what is planted;
a time to kill, and a time to heal;
a time to break down, and a time to build up;
a time to weep, and a time to laugh;
a time to mourn, and a time to dance;
a time to cast away stones, and a time to gather stones together;
a time to embrace, and a time to refrain from embracing;
a time to seek, and a time to lose;
a time to keep, and a time to cast away;
a time to tear, and a time to sew;
a time to keep silence, and a time to speak;
a time to love, and a time to hate;
a time for war, and a time for peace."

Psalm 23

The LORD is my shepherd; I shall not want. He makes me lie down in green pastures. He leads me beside still waters He restores my soul. He leads me in paths of righteousness for his name's sake. Even though I walk through the valley of the shadow of death, I will fear no evil, for you are with me; your rod and your staff, they comfort me. You prepare a table before me in the presence of my enemies; you anoint my head with oil; my cup overflows. Surely goodness and mercy shall follow me all the days of my life, and I shall dwell in the house of the LORD forever.

Matthew 5:4

"Blessed are those who mourn, for they shall be comforted."

There are many more verses like these, but I hope that they will give you some comfort and peace as you go through your trial.

(Right now, I'm sure you know that I am going through a trial as well. I know I posted that the doctor told me I am pregnant, but I am still bleeding, and it's very difficult for me to know for sure whether I'm carrying a baby, whether I'm not carrying a baby, or whether I'm carrying two babies....or if I even miscarried one and have another. I won't know until I get the ultrasound and even then I won't be absolutely certain. It's so hard waiting and not knowing. I completely understand how you feel.)

*I want to add that I do agree with them that you can pray in faith and that miracles can happen. This is Biblical. I simply want to make sure that if the answer to your prayer is not "yes", that you do not blame yourself.

As for your question, what is the baby's purpose....I hope this has helped to answer. I do not think we will always know right away what our babies' purposes are on this earth. I know that our days are numbered from the time we are conceived.... God knows exactly how long each of us will live, even from the very beginning. I don't know what every baby's purpose is (just as I don't know what any other person's purpose is, grown or in the womb), but I do know that God promises that everything happens for a specific purpose, and that we must trust that He knows what He is doing.

Isaiah 55:8-9

"For my thoughts are not your thoughts, neither are your ways my ways, declares the Lord. For as the heavens are higher than the earth, so are my ways higher than your ways and my thoughts than your thoughts. "

If you are wondering if your baby will definitely meet you in Heaven:

Read 2 Samuel Chapter 12. Remember when David and Bathsheba had a baby out of adultery? The baby became sick...while the baby was sick, David prayed to God to spare the baby's life, and would not eat or sleep. As soon as the child was known to have died, David got up, washed his face, and worshiped God. When he was asked why he wasn't mourning the baby anymore, David answered, ". . .I will go to him one day, but he cannot return to me."

Based on this verse, and others which confirm the life and soul of unborn children, I believe that babies do go to Heaven.

I hope that perhaps this has been of some comfort to you. Please let me know if there is anything else I can do....I will pray for you.... please keep me updated on your situation.

July 6, 2007

Can you believe it?

Well, I got the ultrasound today. Guess what I know?

I know no more than I did when I walked in the door to the doctor.

But you know what.... I think I have lost the highly intense emotional state I was in before (at least right now). (The other day I couldn't even walk around for 3 seconds without my eyes brimming with tears).

I don't know if I have just numbed myself down or what, but right now, I am at peace about it. I don't know if I'm pregnant...I don't know if I'm not. I don't know if I was pregnant and miscarried, and I don't know if I miscarried one and there's another one still there.   But right now, I just feel like, I have to find some way to cope and obviously I'm not going to get answers right away, so I'm going to have to deal with it.

The lady who did the ultrasound told me that she could see the uterus, and she showed me what she said was the center of the uterus. She said this is what it looks like usually before you start to see something in pregnancy, and she said that it looked good, and there didn't appear to be anything wrong...but she didn't see a sac, and she didn't see a baby...she didn't see anything. She said that I was still so early that this didn't bother her. She said it didn't necessarily mean that I am not pregnant. I wasn't so sure.

My doctor then told me that they would take some more blood and do some tests on it...and if the levels have gone up, I most likely could still be pregnant. If they've gone down though, she said, unfortunately we both know what that means. She said that the numbers have been confusing, and seeing the ultrasound makes it harder to know for certain what's going on, at least until we see the HCG levels again.

I asked if I could get the levels today possibly...she said yes, and the assistant there told me to call at 4:30, and they should have them in by then. Well, I called at 4:40, and they still didn't have them in. But they told me that they will call me tonight with the results. So tonight, hopefully I will have an update, one way or the other.

I'll be sure to update this post as soon as I know.

JULY 6, 2007

Got the results

It's official.

I'm not pregnant anymore. The levels dropped from 4,400 to 3,077.

This has been one huge roller coaster ride....but at least I finally have a conclusive answer.

The Day I Lost Blessing

I was lying in bed, asleep, at about 2:30 in the morning, when I was awakened by what felt like blood gushing. I realized it was time. Once I felt this, I ran to the bathroom immediately. I felt something coming out...I held it in as I attempted to find something to deliver in. (I couldn't bear to do it on the toilet).

I found a bucket filled with our soap bars, and I dumped it out, then I sat on it. As soon as I had sat down, I felt something pass. The first thing I saw that passed was a blood clot. I picked it up with a tissue, and looked at it, wondering if possibly that was the baby. It was dark red, almost black, and just happened to be in a shape that confused me. At the time, I was scared to throw it away, thinking it actually might be the baby.

Then I happened to look down in the bucket, and realized there was something tiny in there that I had missed. I realized immediately, as soon as I saw it...this was, without a doubt, my baby. There was no mistaking it. (The "gushing" I had felt earlier had apparently been the amniotic sac breaking, and the baby came out separately from the sac).

The baby was the size of a Lima bean, and was gray. I could make out fingers, eyes, I could see the tiny umbilical cord, and I could see the ears. This baby was so intricate and beautiful I could barely believe my eyes. My hands trembled as I tried to figure out how to move it from the bucket. (I was completely unprepared, although I had spent a week on the Internet, researching everything I could find about miscarriage).

I could tell that the baby was very delicate and I was afraid I might destroy it somehow if I wasn't careful.

I gently mopped up all the water and blood inside the bucket, and carefully let the baby slide out of the bucket onto a plastic bag. From there, I carefully picked it up, and stared at it, thinking how absolutely amazing it was.

The moment was so surreal that it was almost as if time had stopped.

Everything was so quiet. It was just me, and the baby.

I remembered that I had decided beforehand that I had purposed to take pictures of the baby...so I grabbed the camera which was in the hallway, with my other hand, which was trembling so hard I could barely hold it steady. The room was dark, so I held my hand right up to the light and took a few pictures.

I took these pictures of the baby in my hand, then put the camera away, and tried to figure out what to do with the baby. I had a jewelry box ready to place the baby in, as a coffin. I had drawn a rose on the box and written on the top, "*Blessing Kerr*".

I had prepared the box with some cotton, but quickly realized that the baby could not lay on the cotton. I laid a piece of plastic over the cotton, laid the baby on top...and not knowing what else to do to preserve the baby, closed the box and put it in the refrigerator, so that I could try to figure out what to do the next day.

When I woke up the next day, I immediately went back to the refrigerator, and realized the baby seemed to be drying out. So I placed the baby into a Ziplock bag of water. My baby had been in amniotic fluid all of his/her life, and I felt like the baby needed to be surrounded in liquid once again before burial. Once I did this, I was astonished that there was even more to this baby than I had previously thought!

I was now able to see the individual fingers, but even more clearly, toes, mouth, tongue, and ears...and I was completely shocked at how beautiful this baby was.

The most amazing part about this is that the baby almost seemed alive, and like it was smiling. This gave me comfort, even though I knew the baby was not really smiling. It's little legs would wiggle in such a lifelike way when the bag moved, and I studied everything from its little spinal cord to the little tiny ears and eyes... it was just so amazing. I was amazed at how absolutely real my baby was. I did not want to forget anything about my baby.

I got the camera out again, got next to a bright window, and took more pictures. I held the bag up against the light and took several pictures. I laid the bag down and took more. I just couldn't' stop staring at my baby. It was just too incredible for words. It astounds me to think that anyone thinks that a baby at this stage of pregnancy (6 weeks) is a blob of tissue. I know for certain that they have no idea what they're talking about.

My husband had been sleeping the entire time I was miscarrying. He didn't even know till the next morning that it had happened at all. I was so fortunate that God spared me physical pain during my miscarriage and also let this happen while everyone was sleeping so that it would be peaceful.

That night, my husband came home with 5 weeping cherry willow trees. He spent a few hours putting the trees in the perfect spot in our yard. Each of 4 trees had its own corner, and the fifth tree was prepared to go into the center. My husband planted the four corner trees first, and after the children had gone to bed, we went out together, to bury our baby under the center tree. We spent about an hour afterward, walking around our house, talking to each other about our feelings, and comforting each other.

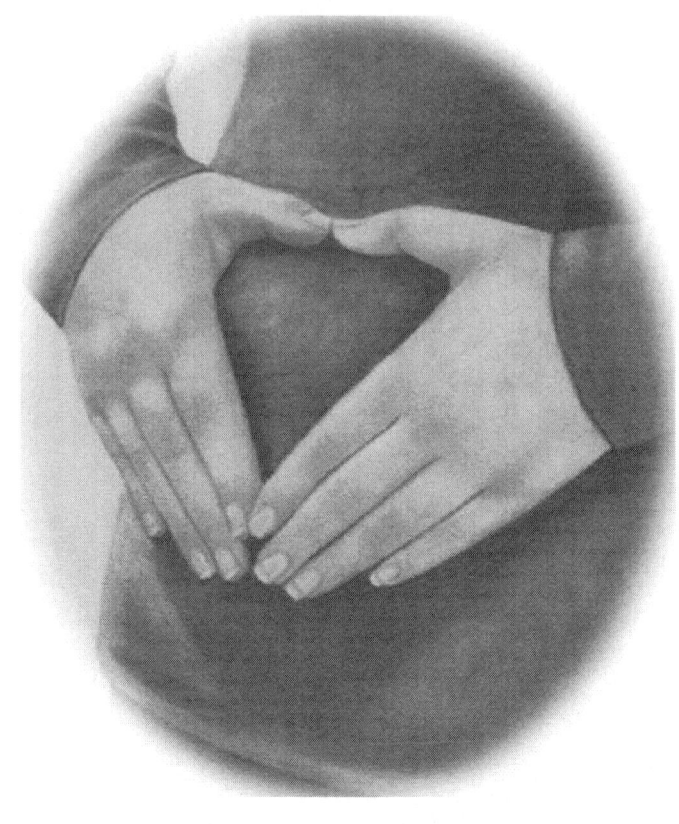

HOW TO COMFORT MOTHERS WHO HAVE
MISCARRIED

WHAT NOT TO SAY

Most of the below comments are well intended but simply misguided efforts to help comfort someone after miscarriage.

- **"It was probably God's way of saying there was something wrong with the baby" or "The baby would have been deformed anyway".**

This answer perpetuates the myth that children are only worth living if they are perfect. The woman grieving most likely would have loved her child no matter what.

- **You're young; you'll be able to have more children.**

This is not comforting to a woman who has just lost her child. Imagine saying this to a woman who just lost a loved one in a car crash or to cancer. The woman who has just lost her child doesn't want to think about having other children right now. *She wants the child she lost.* She needs time to grieve that loss, just as any mother to a born child deserves to grieve her loss before considering having more children.

Ecclesiastes 3:4

"a time to weep, and a time to laugh;
a time to mourn, and a time to dance;"

- **Be thankful for the children you have.**

Of *course* the bereaved mother is grateful for the children who are still living, but remember, she still deserves to grieve her child who she has just lost. Do not make her feel ashamed for the way she feels, and don't try to hurry her through her healing.

- **It's been ___ (amount of time), and aren't you over it yet? It's time to get on with your life.**

It may be difficult for you to see your friend being so sad for long periods of time, and you may be trying to help her cheer up, but you are *not* helping by belittling her pain and telling her to get over it. Pushing her to heal faster is counterproductive as it will only prolong her grief.

- **It could have been worse. You could have lost a baby who was developed further.**

It couldn't have been worse; not for the person who is grieving a loss. Development of the baby has nothing to do with the loss that the mother feels. No matter what stage of development her baby was in, she lost a unique and individual life.

- **I haven't been through what you're going through, but I understand.**

It's okay to say "I can imagine how extremely painful this must be for you", but if you haven't been through the pain of losing your child through miscarriage, please don't pretend to know how it feels.

- **Were you taking your prenatal vitamins?**

Adding unnecessary guilt to the mother is the last thing you need to do at this time. **It is not her fault.** Trying to find the cause is pointless and only makes her feel worse.

Put yourself in her shoes for a moment - Imagine one of your loved ones died; someone you are really close to. When you seek comfort from a friend, the first thing that they say is, "Isn't there something you could have done to prevent it?" It would be hurtful, wouldn't it? You would have been seeking sympathy and compassion, and would have instead been offered the implication that your loved one's death was your fault. Yet, many people don't seem to realize that with miscarriage, it is just as insensitive to do this. Many well intentioned people do and say things they wouldn't say to a woman who lost a born child, a spouse, or a close friend.

If you can't think of anything else to say, the best thing you can do is just to say, "I'm so very sorry for your pain", and then be there for her.

- **At least you know you can get pregnant.**

While that is true, she doesn't know why she couldn't carry her baby to term. Knowing that she *can* get pregnant is the least of her concerns right now. Reminding her she can become pregnant does not help her get over the grief she feels over the baby she lost.

- **It happens all the time/ it's very common, so don't let it bother you.**

Tragedies of *all kinds* are common. That doesn't take away from the pain that they cause to each individual who experiences one.

For example, you could say that newborn babies die *"all of the time"* - does that fact make it any easier on a mother who has lost a newborn? Of course not...so why would this help a woman who has just lost her unborn child?

- **Well, you must be relieved!**

Please do not ever assume that a woman who has lost a baby is relieved. Most women are *not* relieved to have a miscarriage.

It is best to ask the woman herself how she actually is feeling and then be supportive of her when she tells you how she feels.

- **It wasn't even a baby; it was just a blob of cells, clump of tissue, embryo, etc.**

Not only is this one of the most hurtful things that could possibly be said to a woman, it is also wrong.

At fertilization, when the egg and sperm unite, a new individual human being is present with its very own DNA which is different from the mother and fathers. From that moment, a complete human being exists and continues to grow and develop, needing only oxygen, water, and nutrients to develop.

The terms Zygote, Embryo, Fetus, Infant, Toddler, Adolescent, and Adult are all terms to describe different developmental periods in a human beings' lifetime. A zygote is no less human than a toddler because of its stage of development, anymore than a toddler is less human than an adult because of his or her age of development.

When a woman miscarries, she has lost her baby- not just a blob of tissue. [15]

---

[15] *Essentials of Human Embryology*, Toronto B.C. Decker Inc. 1988, L. Shettles, and D. Rovik, *Rites of Life: The Scientific Evidence for Life Before Birth*

- **At least you didn't see (or know) the baby.**

For many women, not seeing/knowing their baby can be the *most* difficult thing about their miscarriage.

- **Well, you can always adopt.**

Your intention may be to cheer her up, but what the mother really needs is for the baby she lost to be acknowledged. Don't change the subject or try to make her think of future babies or children. Yes, she could adopt, but she doesn't want to right now. What she wants is the baby that she lost.

- **When are you going to try again?**

Right after a miscarriage, the last thing she wants to think about is trying again.

In Their Own Words

What didn't help

"As for my friends and extended family ... all gave me kind words the first 2 weeks but after that it just stopped. I was told by one friend that I had demons, one friend got tired of hearing me talk about so I just stopped. Most people I found did not validate a miscarriage as a real "baby" so they could not understand the grief I was feeling. Also, because I had so many other children I was told to be happy and be content by many. Then the shocker came when my own mother many months later told my brother it was time for me to move on and pull myself up by the bootstraps. These comments made me withdraw and stop talking."

- **Shelly Ard**

My husband's cousin and his wife were visiting from out of town. She was pregnant and about a month further along than I would have been. In the course of conversation they asked if we were going to have any more children. We explained that we had just miscarried.
The woman's response was "well I would trade with you in a heartbeat. I wish I would miscarry this baby; it's just so much work! We went to 6-flags today and I rode all the roller coasters, hope that's ok, ha ha." – **Lauren Pope**

"When I was a newlywed 21 years ago, I suffered a miscarriage. I was basically told it was just a glob of cells &

genetic material although it was towards the end of the first trimester. I was told it never would have become a baby.

I'll say...most of the comments really are difficult to hear like "since there was probably something wrong with it, it was for the best" & "you'll have more". I do think the comments are insensitive but many people who say them are well-meaning & they probably don't know what to say. I sometimes feel at a loss for any words (much less eloquent ones) for a situation. Sometimes things come out wrong & one wishes you could take it back & it's awkward to fix the comment after it has been said. I have been guilty of BIG FOOT in mouth disease. So please forgive those who are stumbling for the appropriate thing to say."

-Kay

"I had an early miscarriage--found out I was pregnant one day and miscarried the next. My husband could not believe what I told him that went through my mind about our baby in that 24 hour period. I was thinking about the baby's sex, what room we would put him/her in and lots of other warm thoughts. I felt like no one understood or really even cared. That experience taught me that no matter how early it is--you can be deeply hurt by the loss. A card or note probably would have been nice--just to acknowledge what I was feeling."

-Leigh Anne White

I had a miscarriage between my second and third daughters in 2005, almost exactly 3 years ago. Unfortunately the ones around me didn't know how to handle it and rather hurt me. For one, almost no one even acknowledged my loss. At church no one wanted to say anything about it, I guess for fear of upsetting me, and even family didn't talk to me about it. This really hurt me- I WANTED to talk about it, to acknowledge that I had a child and it died, not just tissue that had to be extracted. (I miscarried at 15 weeks but the baby had been dead for a few weeks and my body wasn't trying to deliver it yet)

No one knew how to help, especially my poor husband. My mom did buy me a book called 'Grieving the child I never knew' and it did help a lot. Talk to the mom about it, acknowledge that she had a baby and is experiencing loss. Talking was what I needed, and no one wanted to listen.

-Jessica Sundholm

I also had a 7 month old at the time and could have really used some help with him. I was so depressed I didn't want to play with him.
I quit enjoying life. I would have loved for someone to say, "Come on, we're going to a movie." I needed someone to drag me out of that house where I sat all day for months with the blinds closed in my PJ's.
I needed some sort of memorial, or closure. I don't know what, but I never got that. A family member had a stillborn baby about 2 weeks after I miscarried (I was 4 months along.) They had a funeral, and as terrible as it may sound, all I could think about being at that funeral, is that I was jealous she had so much support and I had none. I wanted to get the kind of closure she did.

-Tammy

I wish I would have had more support from my own husband. It seems that men don't connect really to the child until they can actually see it. I needed lots of love and support, but didn't get much.

I think people thought if they didn't talk about it then that would be better but I would have loved to talk about it. 3 years later, I still am very careful who I talk to it about it. A lot of close family members feel that maybe it wasn't a baby yet, even though I was almost 6 weeks pregnant. I still think of that little one and the day I lost him. I think about how old he would be, and it is so hard.

I think often people feel that saying nothing at all if better but it is so nice to talk to hear people support you.

-**Sara Newman**

"The hardest thing was probably the callous attitude of the medical "professionals". Everyone was just too perky and too nonchalant. I was grieving and very few people seemed to get that. In addition to the fact that losing a baby that far along is definitely hard on the body, I just needed to be alone for a few days but that was not possible. I remember longing for someone to offer to pick up the children so that I could rest. I was having physical pain but had to go home and cook/clean while hubby was at work..."

"...When people ask me how many children I have I do not really know how to answer. Sometimes I say "6", because I have 6 living children. However, other times I say, "8" because I believe I do have 8. Unfortunately, nearly everyone assumes I lost a baby in infancy when I say something like, "I have 6 here and 2 with Jesus." When people realize that I lost my babies to miscarriage, I usually get a response of, "Oh! I thought you lost a baby." This response is hurtful. My babies were real. They lived a very short time, it's true. But, they were real. They were mine - still are." -**Tera Wolf**

"Many people don't know what to say, but one thing I would say to friends and family is, *"Listen"*.

I've had an awful lot of hurtful comments made to me, and sometimes I just wish that people would realize it's better to just give a hug sometimes then say upsetting things because you're not sure what to say. Try to remember that this isn't something you just "get over"... it stays with a woman her whole life. It can be very hard, especially on anniversaries or family occasions, knowing that a person is missing.

Accept that this baby no matter what age of gestation was a person, that they were loved, missed, and the grief is real. Be aware that a woman who has suffered a miscarriage may not want to hear about other people's pregnancies or be around babies and children for a while sometimes a long time. It's not that they aren't happy for others; it's just extremely hard seeing people having what you have lost.

Talk about their babies with them. Sometimes it feels like everyone has moved on but you, and you feel like no-one cares. By speaking of the lost baby every now and again, they can know that you are still thinking of their little baby, that you care, and that you haven't forgotten."

-**Rebecca Hegarty**

WHAT TO SAY

- I'm so sorry for your loss, and your pain.

- I am praying for you and your family

- If you ever want to talk about it, I am here and will listen.

- This is not your fault. You could have done nothing to prevent this.

- It's okay to grieve.

- I wish I knew what to say or do to make you feel better. I'm here for you though.

- How do you feel? *(then, listen to her if she opens up- give her a hug if needed)*

- Can I bring you dinner?

- Can I watch your kids for a few hours?

- I'm so sad about the baby. I would have loved to have been able to meet him or her. *(It really helps to know that others actually cared about her baby too)*

- Can I help you with the laundry? Dishes?

In their own words

What helped

"There were a lot of healing things that people did and said. My favorite was the "no words hug." Letting me cry for as long as I needed to cry and not saying anything; just holding me. I also appreciated the letters of acknowledgment of my BABY and my loss; I received many poems and a picture of Jesus holding a baby. I framed it. I loved the book I'll Hold You in Heaven (dedicated in memory of my baby). Also, I had friends that remembered the "anniversaries" of the date. Just a call and a card to say they were thinking of me and praying for me. I liked the flowers too.
Practically speaking I loved the dinners that were cooked for us and dropped off. Friends picked up my other children for play dates and allowed my husband and I some time alone. All of these things took the edge off of the insensitive comments I received. People don't want to "bring it up" even though it is all you are thinking about!"

- **Carla Stream**

I have had 2 miscarriages and an ectopic pregnancy in which my tube ruptured and I had major blood loss. All of this has been so hard for me, but what has helped me the most is God. Through my prayers and everyone else's they have really lifted me up and helped me through the rough times. On a more worldly level, though, my friends were a godsend. I had a friend fly from Oklahoma to Florida (where I live) to help me out after I had emergency surgery to remove my ruptured tube. I had friends that called me and cried because they knew how much I wanted that baby. Not that I wanted them to cry, but it really showed that they were genuinely concerned and that they loved me so much!! My family has acted a little weird about all of this, but they still offer their condolences every time.

- **Rheanon Short**

"When I had my first miscarriage, my husband thought he was helping by asking people not to talk to me about it- he hated to see me sad. So his parents and family members didn't say anything. But then we were somewhere and his Aunt whom, we weren't extremely close with came up to me, said she was sorry and gave me a big hug. That was over 13 years ago and I still tear up thinking about her reaching out to me. My co-workers gave me a very touching card and a little guardian angel pin, which is in a special place next to my prom earrings, and some other special jewelry given to me from my grandmother. So I think I am most grateful for those people in my life who acknowledged what an incredible loss it was, even though I wasn't through my first trimester." - **Kristi Bennett**

"...offers to watch children, or do housework, or bring meals are a HUGE help. People don't seem to realize what an adjustment it is for your body and that you NEED time to recoup."

-**Tiffany**

"We lost our baby at 8 weeks gestation. The grief was just overwhelming and nothing could have prepared me for that pain. I think that having people acknowledge that we lost a child was what was most important for me. It wasn't the loss of a 'pregnancy', it was our baby.

Also, even though our loss was an early one, our baby was buried in the family section of our cemetery. Having a place to go and place flowers has been very healing.

Phone calls from well meaning family and friends were just too hard initially. We needed a few days to process what had happened. Also- Now that it has been a year since my miscarriage, it means so much when people speak of our baby to us.

I received a copy of John Macarthur's, *"Safe in the Arms of God"*. It was wonderful and so helpful. Anything that can be used to remember is very special - a plant, a piece of jewelry, a figurine. Any gift given out of love and concern is much appreciated!"

–Jane

"Probably one of the most important things you can do to a friend who lost a baby at birth is to mention the baby's name often- don't be afraid to say the name just because you know tears will well up in my eyes- it means you care and loved my baby too if you remember my baby's name!!, remember the baby's birthday (whether the baby was only 9 weeks along or full term) remembering the date is very important and it doesn't take much to show you remember- just a short visit and a hug or a card, flowers, or a small gift.

Another gift that blessed and overwhelmed us was a gift certificate for a get away to a bed and breakfast for the two of us (our wedding anniversary is the day after one of our son's birthdays) and with the birth/death of our son the day before we spent our anniversary night in the hospital so our anniversary wasn't celebrated like we would have wanted to celebrate it. Several months later we used the gift and had a wonderful time of refreshment and relaxation!"

-**Cris**

"What has helped me the most is reading other women's stories. Miscarriage makes you feel so alone; you feel like it is your fault. Reading other women's stories helps you realize that you are not alone. I have found it is much easier to talk to someone about miscarriage when they have been through it themselves. Someone who has never been through it just doesn't understand. I sometimes get the comments..."It wasn't meant to be", "It had something wrong with it", "there is nothing you can do about it now", "be thankful you have one child", and be thankful you weren't further along"...The list goes on. I know some people don't know what to say...But I would rather complete silence and a hug rather than an insensitive comment that only makes me feel worse. The best thing for me has also been to share my story with other angel mommies.

I think Jewelry is an appropriate gift for a grieving mother; perhaps the birthstone of when your baby was to born, or was born; an angel pin, something you can wear close to your heart.

–Lindsey

I feel like after a couple of months, people forgot. I know they didn't, but I just wish that people would have felt comfortable to ask me how I was doing. Another thing that really bothers me, being pregnant again, is when people act like it is my "first." This is my second baby and nothing will ever change that.

My favorite gift that I received was a pearl necklace from my aunt. She said that just as the Lord made that pearl, He created our little one so perfectly and that I could wear this as a reminder. I have not taken it off since the day I got it. Another gift which I loved was a bag of homemade cookies and a CD with songs of comfort - that really ministered to my grieving heart.

- Marcie

"I was really upset with the people said nothing (ie no card - no call - kept their distance).... I know they did not know what to say - and many people did put their foot in it and said terrible things like "there probably never really was a real baby but just a mass of malformed cells" - but still they came and said something. I loved it when people came and just listened to me rabble on and cry and rabble on and cry.
I had fantastic practical support from the church, who looked after my 3 children, and brought meals etc (I had an ectopic and the operation left me in bed for weeks in agony). I can't thank them enough for their help.

The people I appreciate most are the few who just sat with me and let me talk, talk, and talk. They needn't have said anything – what helped me most was their willingness to listen.

Another thing a friend said which was really, really helpful (they had lost a baby boy at 24 weeks a few years ago) was "Don't panic about how you feel. Don't feel like you have to pull yourself together and not cry - and don't feel guilty when you laugh - or smile at something... Don't even feel guilty when you feel nothing at all - grief is a process."

I found this particularly helpful as I did feel awful when for a split second I forgot my grief, and laughed at one of my other children doing something funny. I suppose I had felt that I had cheated her memory."

-Jennie Lee

There was a CD that I listened to a lot when I first became pregnant with my baby who is in Heaven now. It still has a comfort, but also sadness, when I listen to it. It is just a classical piano CD, but I pulled it out the other day and all the memories came back to me and I felt the pain again. It still makes me remember the baby I lost. I didn't really read any books at the time but I had lots of online support. It was so nice to hear other women that went through or were going through the same thing.

There was one lady in particular that was very comforting and that was a lady named Sandi...a few years earlier, she had went through the same thing. She was actually talking to me on the day I had to wait so long to hear the news from the doctor. She sent me such comforting words. I am forever grateful for all that she did that day.

I think one of the hardest things I had to do was when I had to tell others that I lost the baby. That was so hard...it got to the point that I couldn't, and I had to have John tell them. I taught piano at the time and I wanted to take a little break off. I was trying to call people and let them know... and I got through a few phone calls but couldn't continue, so John had to finish it for me. The words are so hard to say out loud: "I lost my baby"

-**Sara Newman**

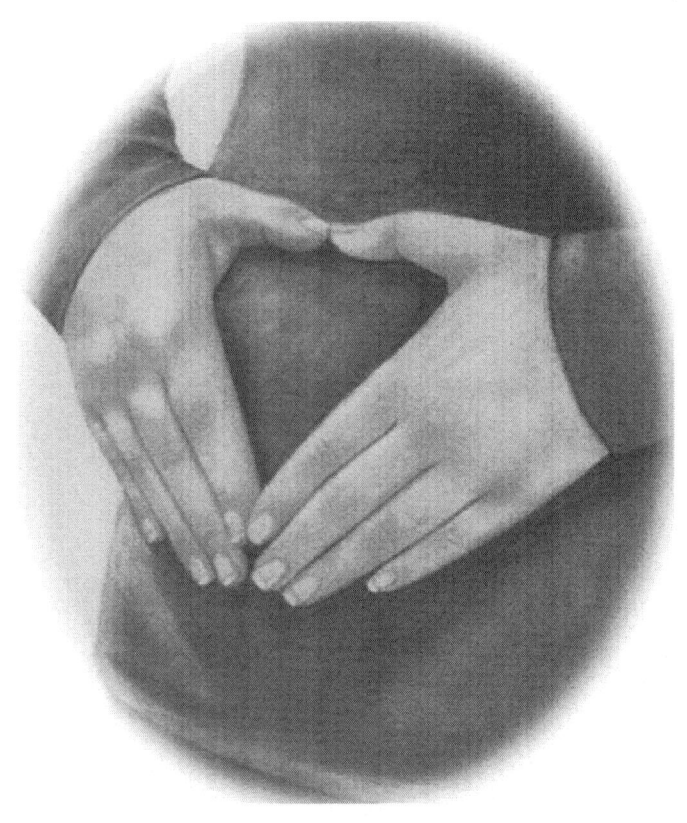

ENCOURAGEMENT

Poems

Miss You Every Day

"Each day is another chance to say good-bye to you, our precious baby.

Ever since I saw the positive pregnancy test, I have loved you, little one. I couldn't help it.

Even though I knew the chances were not good that you would live to full term, I loved each day God gave me with you.

You are a precious soul and I will see you in heaven someday. It's a long time to get to heaven and I'll miss you every day.

My prayer ever since I knew about you was that your life would glorify God, and it did in many special ways.

Your life has touched and changed mine and your Daddy's. Your brothers and sisters loved you from when they first heard about you too. They had many tears of sadness when we learned of the loss of your life.

We do not understand God's reasons for taking you before we could see you and hold you. I would have loved to see your beautiful face, nurse you, and smell your heavenly smell. I would have loved to know if you were a boy or a girl.

Your life was proof of God's love for our family. What joy your little life gave to all of us! Every day these past few weeks, were filled with thankfulness to God and awe at the gift of you!

As a small wildflower hidden on a mountainside with no one to see it besides God, your life was hidden away from all human eyes. God knew you and formed each part of you.

You are precious to Him and were made for His glory. I cling to that fact and take comfort in it. As I write this, your body is still inside mine. I touch my stomach, wishing I could reach you, and I want to remember every detail of this pregnancy.

My body welcomed you and we wanted you very much. You were created for God's pleasure and I know you are with Him right now.

I say good-bye to you with trust in God's faithfulness. His ways are higher than mine and His plans and purposes are perfect. God gives and God takes away, but I praise and trust Him always.

With all my love,

Mommy" - **Melanie Kendall**

A Pair of Shoes

I am wearing a pair of shoes.
They are ugly shoes.
Uncomfortable shoes.
I hate my shoes.

Each day I wear them, and each day I wish I had another pair.
Some days my shoes hurt so bad that I do not think I can take another step.
Yet, I continue to wear them.

I get funny looks wearing these shoes.
They are looks of sympathy.
I can tell in others eyes that they are glad they are my shoes and not theirs.
They never talk about my shoes.

To learn how awful my shoes are might make them uncomfortable.
To truly understand these shoes you must walk in them.
But, once you put them on, you can never take them off.
I now realize that I am not the only one who wears these shoes.

There are many pairs in this world.
Some woman are like me and ache daily as they try and walk in them.
Some have learned how to walk in them so they don't hurt quite as much.

Some have worn the shoes so long that days will go by before they think about how much they hurt.

No woman deserves to wear these shoes.
Yet, because of these shoes I am a stronger woman.
These shoes have given me the strength to face anything.

They have made me who I am.
I will forever walk in the shoes of a woman who has lost a child.

Author unknown

Always My Baby

You were not planned, but how I wanted you.
You were not held, but I touched you.
You were called an embryo, but I called you my baby.
You no longer had a heartbeat, but my heart still beat for you.
You may be gone, but I will never forget you.
You now live with your sister, but I am your family too.
You never got to know me, but I knew you.
No, you were not planned, but oh how I loved you.

by Nancy Van De Vaarst

(You may contact Nancy at <u>vandevaa@us.ibm.com</u>.)

My Son

In a baby castle just beyond our eye
Our baby plays with angel toys that money cannot buy
Who are we to wish you back
Into this world of strife?
No Jack play on baby
You have eternal life
At night when all is silent
And sleep forsakes our eyes
We hear your tiny footsteps
Come running to our side
Your little hands caress us
So tenderly and sweet
We'll breathe a prayer and close our eyes
And embrace you in our sleep.

-"Cookie"

<u>Jamie</u>
Our family was soon
to be three.
Patrick and I and
the baby in me.
There was no heartbeat.
How could this be true?
There was fear.
There was pain.
Then I held you.
You had lived in me
10 weeks and 6 days.
Now I don't care what
anyone says.
Their ignorance hurts.
They can't feel what we feel.
If only they would acknowledge
that our Jamie was real.
Now you live in heaven without us.
Our little angel is home
safe with Jesus.

In loving memory of Jamie Stream
From Mom and Dad, October 1995

ARTICLES

Blessed by Sorrow

We each walk a different path and we are each shaped by our past experiences. Each of us has experienced some sort of tragedy or heartache in our lives but it is often what we take from it that makes the most impact on how we live.

Some folks choose to live with bitterness whether it is towards those who have wronged them or towards God. This bitterness eats away at them and robs their peace and their joy.

Some folks choose to apply a Band-Aid in the hopes that their pain will go away – but it never does and they are left with a feeling of emptiness and hopelessness.

Then there are those who trust in the Lord and believe that He has set their feet upon their current path and they are going to follow Him, no matter the cost.

I like to think of myself as 'one of those people'. I certainly have my share of times when I trust in myself, but I have learned that the Lord doesn't send us down a path for no reason. Often, He sends us down a path so that we can turn around and help others who come along behind us.

Suddenly, through our own pain, we are blessed. The love that the Lord has for us becomes more vivid and through the ache of our heart and the sting of our tears, we can feel His comforting embrace.

We often don't know why we may experience pain and

tragedy but we have to trust in the Lord. We serve a mighty God, a good God and a loving God. He truly desires the best for us – but sometimes His plan doesn't make us happy. We simply have to realize that we may not understand His ways but if we are to have true peace and joy (not the same as happiness) we have to trust Him and yield our will to His.

This afternoon as I was reading in my Bible the Lord spoke to me in such an awesome way. I started reading in Ecclesiastes 7, and while I enjoyed the whole passage, verse 3 really blessed me: "Sorrow is better than laughter; for by the sadness of the countenance the heart is made better."

Life isn't all about happiness and pleasure (laughter). There are times when we must bear sorrow. It has been through my deepest sorrow that I have come to know the Lord on a deeper level and it has been that sorrow that has helped me see the true worth of the precious gift of Jesus' shed blood. My own personal sorrow has made me stronger and it has deepened my compassion for others.

As I walk down my path in life, I will meet many on the same journey that I am on. God has sent me ahead of some of these so that I can shine His light on them as they go through the dark valley.

What have you been through and how can you use these sorrows to bring glory and honor to the Lord? How can you bless others by simply being someone that they can look to and see how the Lord has brought you through and in doing so, encourage them that the Lord will bring them through?

If you are stuffing your sorrow down instead of growing through it and blessing others through, then you are missing out on a great blessing. It might take stepping out of your comfort zone, but remember that God is the one who has set you on this path and you have the ability to make a positive difference in lives of others.

–**Dana Patterson**

Glory to God

"My youngest daughter lovingly brought me a pretty wild sunflower she had picked from beside the road at my parents' farm. "Here you go, Mommy. It's for you!" she said as she handed it to me. I looked at the pretty yellow flower and thought of the hundreds of flowers growing beside the roads all over the countryside where my parents live. I was glad she had brought it to my notice and wanted to share it with me.

These flowers are barely noticed and are taken for granted by busy adults that pass by them. Each of these flowers and all the many varieties of wild flowers that grow on mountainsides, in meadows, and along country roads all over our world were created by God, and are for His glory. Many of them are never even seen or appreciated by human eyes, but God sees each of them and takes pleasure in them all.

As I looked at the wild sunflower and its delicate, lovely petals, God brought to my mind the precious, delicate little life that has been growing in my womb. Its life has never been seen by any human, and only a small number of people have even known of its existence. Now that life has ended at only a few weeks. In my sadness, God speaks to me saying that its life was not in vain, that it brought glory to Him and was His creative work. He planned each day of its life, and knew it before it was even conceived. Its life gave
our family much joy from the moment we knew of its existence, and we praised God for His gift.

As my baby's life was short and fleeting, like a wildflower's, it was beautiful and had a purpose. I thank God for this reminder so lovingly brought to me by Him to comfort me in my grief and sadness".- **Melanie Kendall**

Quotes

"Even when there is chaos in our lives, we can experience indescribable peace because we know that whatever we are going through, God already knows about it and has equipped us to handle it with His grace. It is His faithfulness that gives up confidence and peace."
-Thelma Wells

"Trials are medicines which our gracious and wise Physician prescribes because we need them; and he proportions the frequency and weight of them to what the case requires. Let us trust his skill and thank him for his prescription."
 - Isaac Newton

"We can decide to let our trials crush us, or we can convert them to new forces of good"

- Helen Keller

When a baby arrives,
be it for a day, a month, a year or more,
or perhaps only a sweet flickering moment-
the fragile spark of a tender soul
the secret swell of a new pregnancy
the goldfish flutter known to only you-
you are unmistakably changed...
the tiny footprints left behind on your heart
bespeak your name as Mother.

-Kimberly de Montbrun

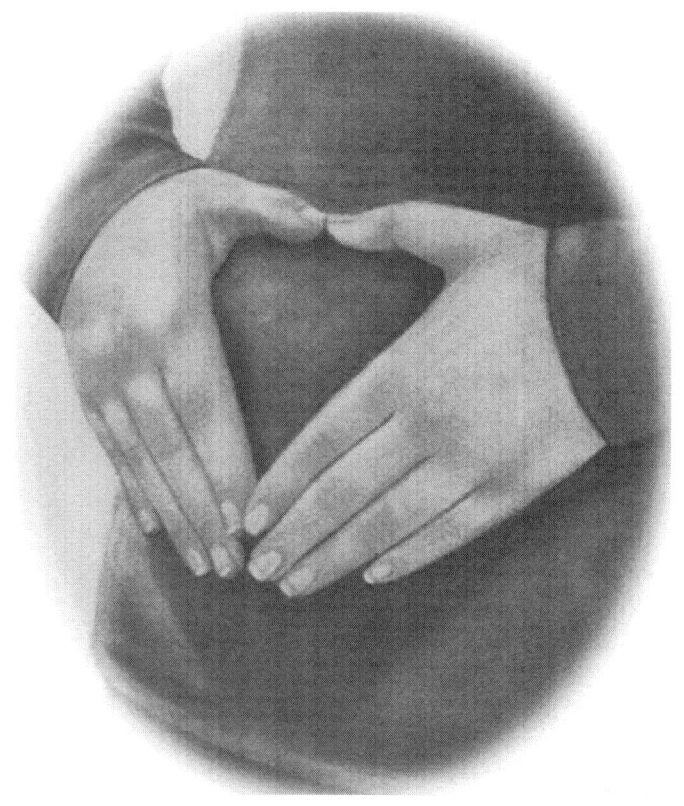

Resources

Books

Here are some titles of books that have helped me, or that have been recommended by other grieving moms:

Empty Arms: Emotional Support for Those Who Have Suffered Miscarriage or Stillbirth

By Pam Vredevelt

(this book also includes help for those suffering after ectopic (tubal) pregnancy)

I'll Hold You in Heaven (Remembrance Book)

By Debbie Heydrick

Safe in the Arms of God: Truth from Heaven About the Death of a Child

By John Macarthur

Grieving the Child I Never Knew

By Kath Wunnenberg

(You can read this book online for free. Just type the title in the search engine (Google) to find it).

Teardrop Diary: A journal with poetry for healing your heart after pregnancy loss.

By Erin McSparron.

The Littlest S.I.R.

By Loretta Rizzo

You can purchase this book at: http://www.lulu.com/hispen

Or send $10.00 to: *Loretta Rizzo, P. O. Box 3921, Kingman, AZ 86402-3921*

Life Line: A Journal for Parents Grieving a Miscarriage, Stillbirth, or Other Early Infant Death

By Jeanie Reid

Miscarriage: A Quiet Grief

By Kraybill, Nelson, and Ellen Kraybill

Miscarriage: A Shattered Dream

Linda Hammer Burns

Miscarriage: A Man's Book

By Rick Wheat

Mommy, Please Don't Cry

By Linda DeYmaz

Silent Grief

By Clara Hinton

We Were Gonna Have a Baby, But We Had an Angel Instead

By Pat Schwiebert.

(A book to help parents *and* children understand loss of their child/sibling)

Miscarriage: Women Sharing from the Heart

By Marie Allen and Shelly Marks.

Our Stories of Miscarriage: Healing With Words

By Rachel Fadet

WEBSITES

Facts about Miscarriage

http://pregnancyloss.info/

Comfort in Heaven (discussion group)

http://www.comfortinheaven.com

Misdiagnosed Miscarriage (discussion group)

http://www.misdiagnosedmiscarriage.com

(Although this site is titled *"Misdiagnosed* Miscarriage", it is a forum for women who have actually had all types of miscarriages, and is one of the most supportive and loving groups I've found).

Ectopic Pregnancy

http://www.ectopicpregnancy.com/

Little Angels Online Store

http://www.littleangelsonlinestore.com/

Share- Pregnancy and Infant Loss Support Inc.

http://www.nationalshareoffice.com/

A Place to Remember

http://www.aplacetoremember.com/

Remembering Them

http://www.rememberingthem.net/

This Girl Will Never be the Same

http://thisgirl-amanda.blogspot.com/

Silent Grief

http://silentgrief.com/

Endowment for Human Development

http://www.ehd.org/

Songs

"I Would Die for That"

By Kellie Coffey

"Bring on the Rain"

Jo Dee Messina

Praise You in This Storm

Casting Crowns

"I Know You Were my Son"

Jaydeen Georgeff

"Fly"

Celine Dion

"Angels Among Us"

Alabama

"I Give to You His Heart"

Alison Krauss

"If I Die Young"

The Band Perry

"Glory Baby"

Watermark

"Hello, Goodbye"

Michael W. Smith

"With Hope"

Steven Curtis Chapman

"Trust His Heart"

Babbie Mason

"Tears in Heaven"

Eric Clapton

"To Where You Are"

Josh Groben

"Held"

Natalie Grant

"Slipped Away"

Avril Lavigne

Scripture

Proverbs 3:5-6…"Trust in the Lord with all your heart, and do not lean on your own understanding. In all your ways acknowledge him, and he will make straight your paths "

Isaiah 41:10…"Fear not, for I am with you; be not dismayed, for I am your God; I will strengthen you, I will help you, I will uphold you with my righteous right hand."

Matthew 5:4-12 …"And he opened his mouth and taught them, saying: Blessed are the poor in spirit, for theirs is the kingdom of heaven. Blessed are those who mourn, for they shall be comforted. Blessed are the meek, for they shall inherit the earth. Blessed are those who hunger and thirst for righteousness, for they shall be satisfied. Blessed are the merciful, for they shall receive mercy. Blessed are the pure in heart, for they shall see God. Blessed are the peacemakers, for they shall be called sons of God."

James 1:12 …"Blessed is the man who remains steadfast under trial, for when he has stood the test he will receive the crown of life, which God has promised to those who love him."

Romans 5:3-5 …"More than that, we rejoice in our sufferings, knowing that suffering produces endurance, and endurance produces character, and character produces hope, and hope does not put us to shame, because God's love has been poured into our hearts through the Holy Spirit who has been given to us."

Romans 8:16,17..."The Spirit himself bears witness with our spirit that we are children of God, and if children, then heirs—heirs of God and fellow heirs with Christ, provided we suffer with him in order that we may also be glorified with him."

II Corinthians 4:8-9..."We are hard pressed on every side, yet not crushed; we are perplexed, but not in despair; persecuted, but not forsaken; struck down, but not destroyed."

II Corinthians 12:10 ... "For the sake of Christ, then, I am content with weaknesses, insults, hardships, persecutions, and calamities. For when I am weak, then I am strong."

II Timothy 1:7..."for God gave us a spirit not of fear but of power and love and self-control."

I John 2:15-17..."Do not love the world or the things in the world. If anyone loves the world, the love of the Father is not in him. For all that is in the world—the desires of the flesh and the desires of the eyes and pride in possessions—is not from the Father but is from the world. And the world is passing away along with its desires, but whoever does the will of God abides forever. "

Hebrews 4:16..."Let us then with confidence draw near to the throne of grace, that we may receive mercy and find grace to help in time of need."

Psalm 42:5-6a..."Why are you cast down, O my soul, and why are you in turmoil within me? Hope in God; for I shall again praise him, my salvation and my God. My soul is cast down within me; therefore I remember you."

Psalm 138:3..."On the day I called, you answered me; my strength of soul you increased. "

1 Peter 1:6…"In this you rejoice, though now for a little while, if necessary, you have been grieved by various trials."

Psalm 22:24…"For he has not despised or abhorred the affliction of the afflicted, and he has not hidden his face from him, but has heard, when he cried to him. "

Matthew 5:4…"Blessed are those who mourn, for they shall be comforted."

1 Peter 5:7…"so that the tested genuineness of your faith—more precious than gold that perishes though it is tested by fire—may be found to result in praise and glory and honor at the revelation of Jesus Christ."

Proverbs 31:25…"Strength and dignity are her clothing, and she laughs at the time to come."

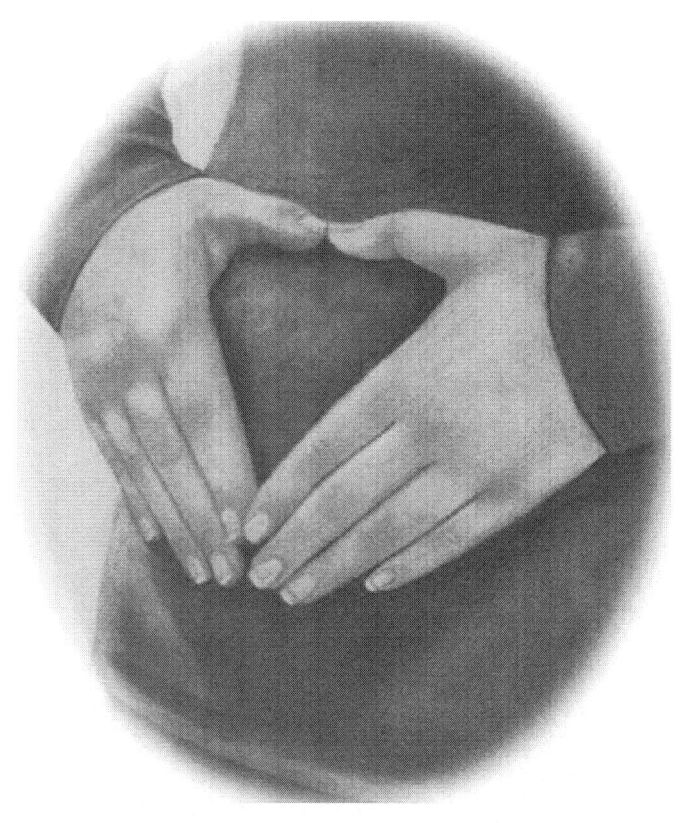

FETAL DEVELOPMENT

Seven Weeks

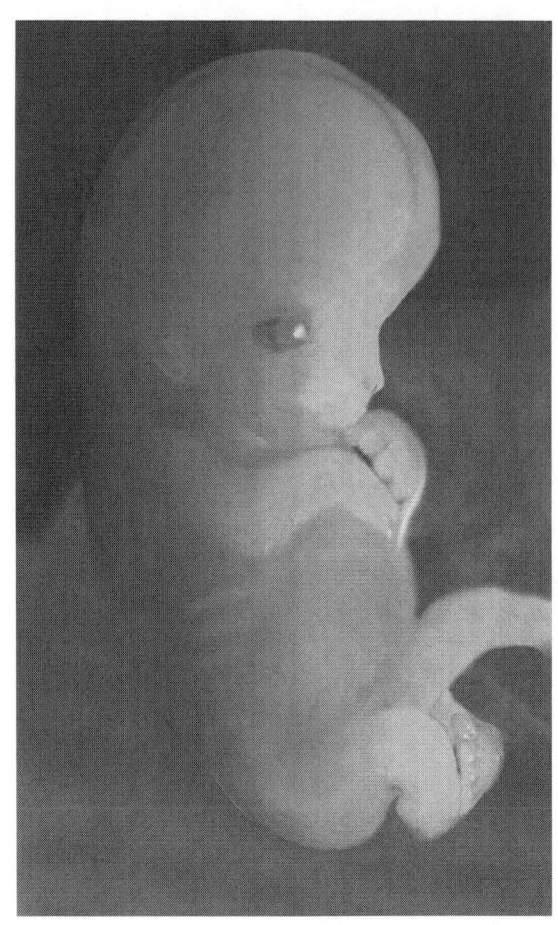

Eight Weeks

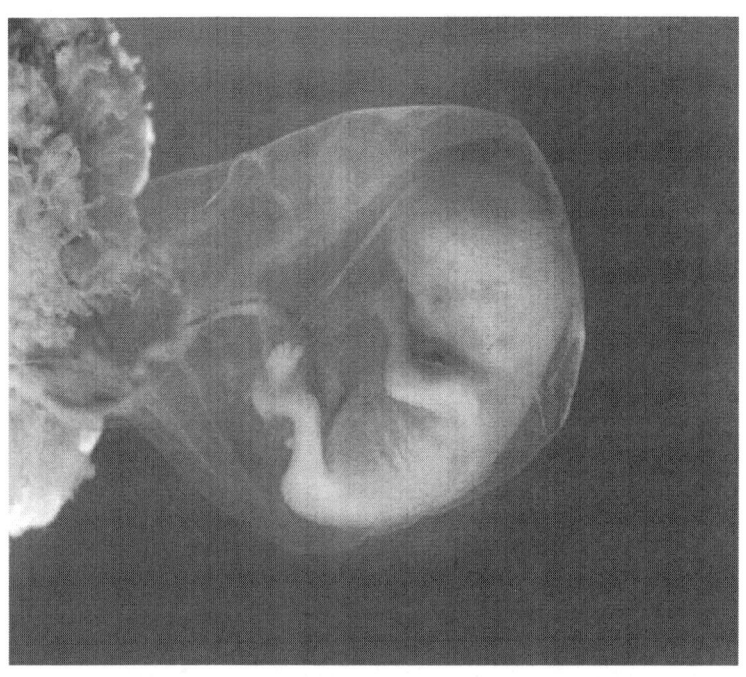

Eleven Weeks

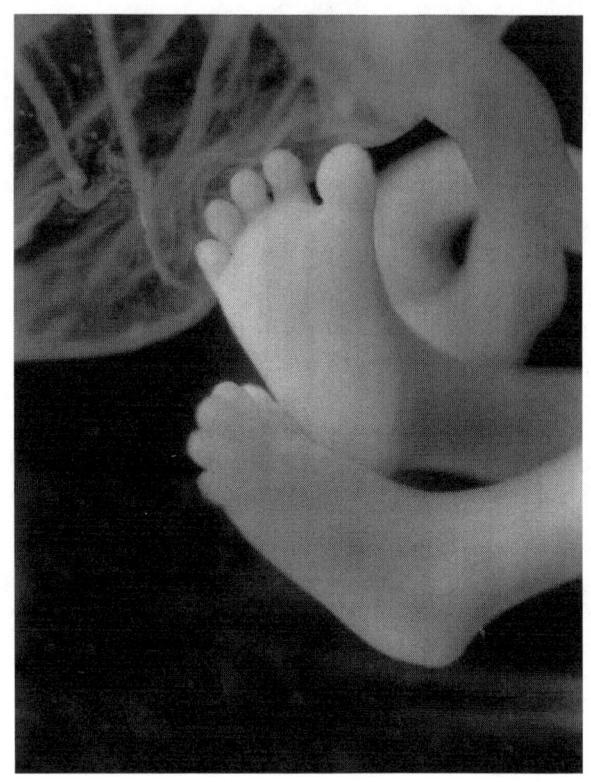

Twenty Weeks

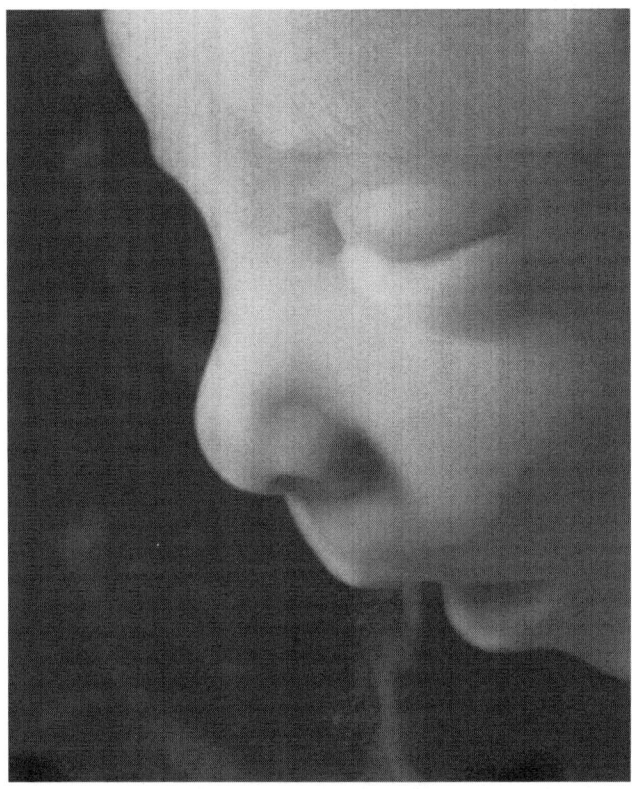

Photos courtesy of Professor Andrzej Skawina (Collegium Medicum Jagiellonian University, Krakow) and Dr. Antoni Marsinek, MD (Czerwiakowski Gynecological and Obstetrics Hospital, Krakow) who made these images available for public use, and the Zrodlo Foundation, Wychowawca Department.

Rowan's Funeral Pictures
(read story on pages 41 and 60)

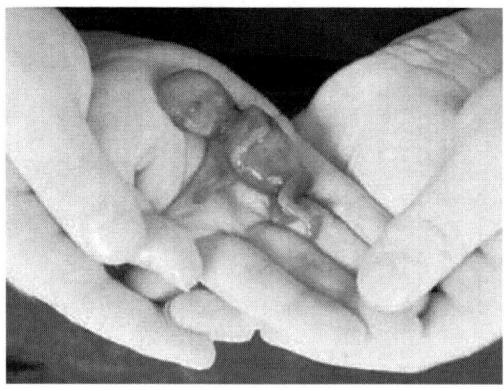

Pictures of My Baby, Blessing Kerr

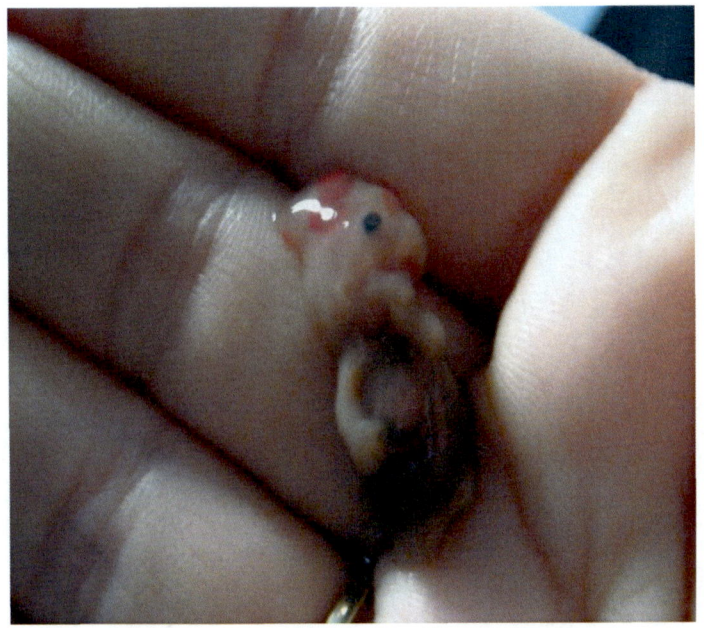

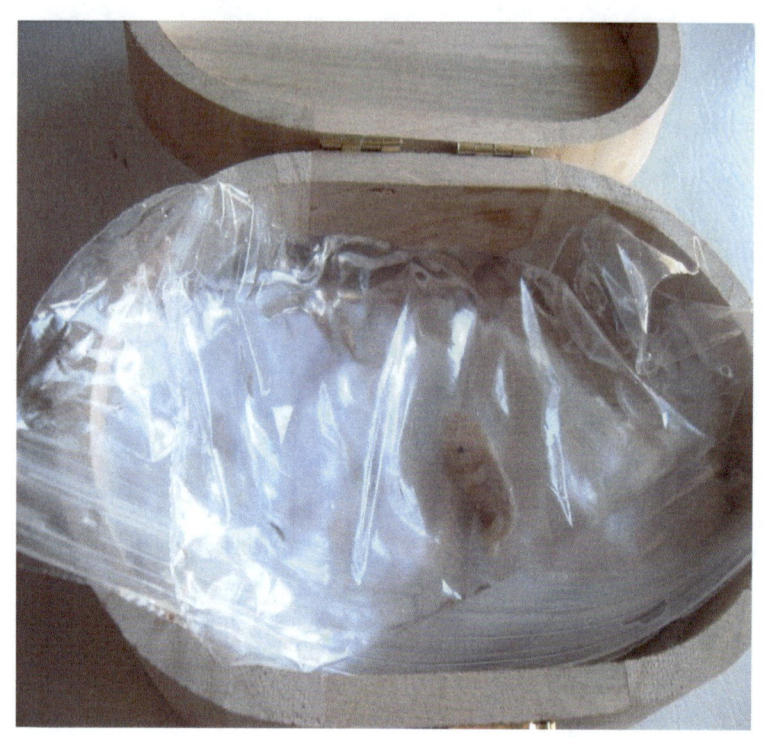

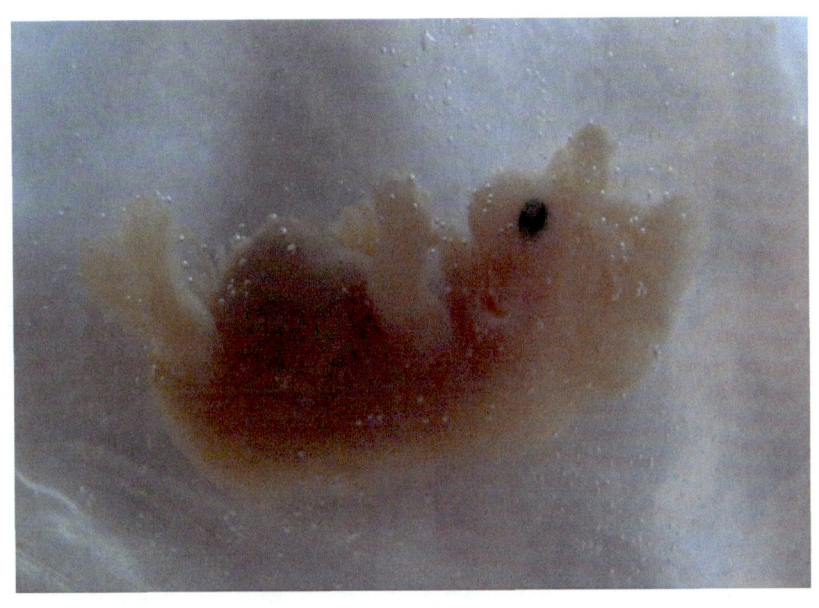

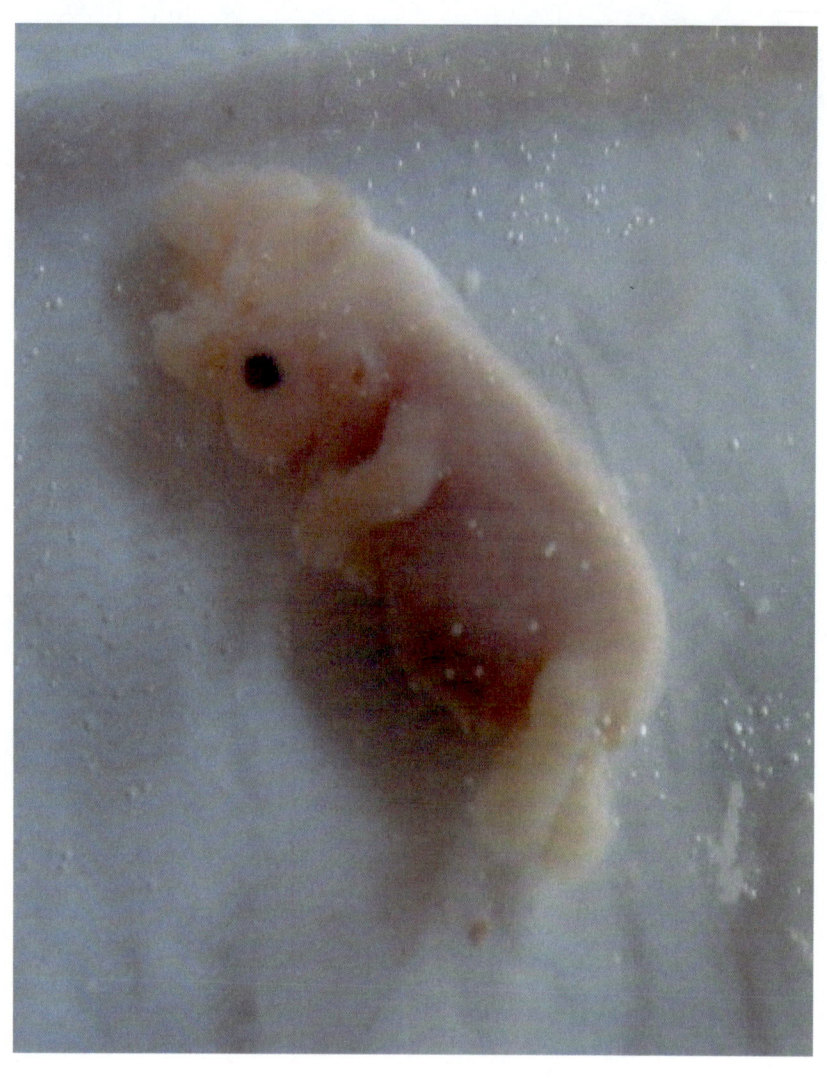

About the Author

Bethany Kerr is a follower of Christ, married to her beloved for 12 years, mother of four with another on the way, talented artist, and gifted writer. She has been blogging for years, with a focus on motherhood and faith. After suffering two miscarriages in 2007, Bethany was inspired to share her heart with others who have experienced losses through this book. Bethany makes her home in Alabama, where she homeschools her children and continues her artistic pursuits. Her portraits grace the walls of many homes and her murals can be found on several local buildings. [16]

http://www.sketchesbybethany.net |
http://bethany.preciousinfants.com

---

[16] Written by Margaret Delle from http://homeschoolblogger.com/cappuccinosmom/

To order additional copies of this book, send this order form with check or money order to:

Attn: Bethany Kerr
Silver Trumpet Publishing
801 County Road 1609
Cullman, Alabama 35058

Product	Price	Quantity	Subtotal
Answers in a Time of Miscarriage book	$14.95		
Shipping and Handling	$3.00		

If you are ordering 5 or more books, the price per book will be $11.95.

Your shipping address:

Name: _____

Address: _____

City, State, Zip: _____

Telephone (optional):_____

Email (optional)_____